The MAS[illegible] KIDS' JOKE BOOK

The MASSIVE KIDS' JOKE BOOK

Collected and Illustrated by

PETER COUPE

ARCTURUS

Published by
Arcturus Publishing Limited
For
Bookmart Limited
Registered Number 2372865
Desford Road
Enderby
Leicester
LE9 5AD

This edition published 2001

Printed and bound by Omnia Books limited

Cover by Chris Smith

Edited by John Maxwell

Proof-read by Rebecca Panayiotou

Design by Zeta Fitzpatrick @ Moo

ISBN 1-84193-070-9

Arcturus Publishing Limited
1-7 Shand Street
London SE1 2ES

Contents...

STUPID SCHOOLDAYS

Why did the maths teacher take a ruler in his car ?

So he could see how long it took him to get to work in the morning !

I hope you aren't going to spend the whole lesson watching the clock !

Certainly not, Sir. I have my alarm set for 3.45, and I'm hoping to get a little nap later !

What do you shout when Santa Claus does the register ?

Present !

I thought you were going to play school with me today!

I did - I decided to play absent!

What do you do if someone faints in a maths exam?

Try to bring them 2!

Parent - Why have you given my little boy such a bad report - he's as intelligent as the next boy!

Teacher - Yes, but the next boy is an idiot!

Why are you taking that sponge into your lesson?

I always find History such an absorbing subject!

Did you hear about the maths teacher who was thrown out of the pizza restaurant - for asking how long his pizza would be?

Vicar - Can anyone tell me what Samson did for a living ?

Pupil - I think he was a comedian - it says in the Bible that he brought the house down !

✎

Why does your teacher have her hair in a bun ?

Because she has a face like a burger !

✎

Why do teachers never marry dairy farmers ?

They are like chalk and cheese !

✎

Why do doctors enjoy their schooldays ?

Because they are good at examinations !

✎

So, Blenkinsop, you claim to know all your tables - let's hear them then !

Dining Room table, Kitchen table, Living Room table........

COLLECTIVE NOUNS....

A NUMBER of maths teachers !

A RANGE of cookery teachers !

A TEAM of P.E. teachers !

A CONCENTRATION of science teachers !

A BAND of music teachers !

A FOREST of woodwork teachers !

A BANK of economics teachers !

A SCHOOL of headteachers !

Teacher - Sally, give me a sentence with the word aroma in it !

Sally - My uncle Fred is always travelling, he's aroma !

✎

What did the ghostly music teacher play ?

Haunting melodies !

✎

Why do vampire teachers not like computers ?

They hate anything new fangled !

✎

The maths teacher is feeling run down today !

Wow ! Did anyone get the number of the car that did it !

✎

What happens to a maths teacher's class when he retires ?

Before or after you've woken them up ?

LET ME INTRODUCE THE FAMILY...

The maths teacher's son - Juan !

The music teacher's daughters - Melody and Carol !

The woodwork teacher's daughter - Giselle !

The caretaker's daughter - Mona !

The computer teacher's son - Chip !

✎

Now - just settle down you lot !
I don't come into this classroom to
listen to this sort of racket !

Oh - where do you usually go, Miss ?

✎

What is the plural of mouse ?

Mice !

What is the plural of house ?

Hice !

I call my first year class my little treasures -

because goodness only knows where they were dug up !

Why do history teachers like fruit cake ?

Because it's full of dates !

Headteacher - Mr Phelps, do you have any sawdust ?

Mr Phelps - No, Head, all my dust is perfectly healthy thank you !

My maths teacher is a real peach!

You mean she's pretty?

No - I mean she has a heart of stone!

✎

Teacher - I'd like a ticket to Cambridge please!

Travel Agent - Single sir?

Teacher - No, actually I'm married to Miss Whelk the Chemistry teacher!

✎

Teacher - Clark, have you been an idiot all your life?

Clark - Not yet, Sir!

✎

We can't possibly play football out there - the pitch is wet through!

I know - the first years have been doing dribbling practise all morning!

John - what is the plural of baby ?

Twins !

Give me a sentence with the word politics in it !

**Our parrot swallowed the alarm clock,
and now politics !**

In the Bible it tells us that God was a healer !

I know that, Sir, because he gave Moses some tablets !

If you multiply 245 by 3456 and divide the answer by 165, then subtract 752, what will you get ?

The wrong answer, Miss !

✎

What's the difference between a train and a teacher ?

A train says "choo - choo" but a teacher says "take that gum out of your mouth this instant !"

✎

Why did the scruffy schoolboy finally take a bath ?

Because he realised that grime doesn't pay !

✎

Blenkinsop - your parents are multi-millionaires, and yet you still smell awful !

That's because we're filthy rich, Miss !

✎

Inspector - How many teachers work in this school ?

Pupil - Very few !

How do you make a sick insect better ?

Give it a T, then it will be a stick insect !

Why are some snakes really good at maths ?

They are adders !

What do history teachers do before they get married ?

They go out on dates !

Who teaches all the boys called Ed ?

The Ed teacher !

I didn't use a recipe for this casserole -
I made it out of my own head!

I thought it tasted of sawdust!

✎

Why are you always late for school?

Because I threw my alarm clock in the bin!

Why on earth did you do that?

It kept going off when I was still asleep and waking me up!

✎

Where do vampire schoolchildren go for field trips?

Lake Eerie!

✎

Why are you scratching yourself boy?

Because no-one else knows where I itch!

Blenkinsop, where is Turkey ?

No idea, Sir, we threw ours away after Christmas !

I think our school must be haunted - because teacher keeps going on about the school spirit !

Blenkinsop, are you any good at History ?

Well, Miss, to be honest, yes and no !

What do you mean yes and no ?

I mean, yes, I'm no good at History !

Blenkinsop – if I were to borrow £100 from your father, and he paid me back at a rate of £10 per month, how much would he owe me after 6 months ?

£100, Sir !

Oh, dear, Blenkinsop, I'm afraid you don't know much about maths do you ?

And you don't know much about my father !

✎

Violin for sale – going cheap – no strings attached !

✎

Why did the teacher pick Snodgrass to be teacher's pet ?

Because he is the person who looks most like her dog !

✎

I'm sorry, Mr Cyclops, I don't think you are suited to teaching – you only have the one pupil !

What has 22 legs, is dripping wet and sings out of tune ?

The school football team in the showers after a match !

✎

What sort of vampire is attracted to music and soldiers ?

A sharp major !

✎

How many millions of times have I told you, Blenkinsop, stop exaggerating !

✎

Why did the music teacher ban skeletons from keyboard lessons ?

They have no organs !

✎

Why is that boy locked up in a cage in the corner of the classroom ?

Oh, he's the teacher's pet !

Please, Miss, I've swallowed my pencil sharpener!

You must be choking!

No, Miss, I'm perfectly serious!

This school pie has hairs in it!

That's odd – it says rabbit pie on the menu!

The teacher said that you weren't fit to be with pigs – but I stood up for you!

Really, what did you say?

I said that you were!

There once was a schoolboy called Pete,

Who stuck coloured pens on his feet.

Now where ever he goes,

If he wiggles his toes,

He can draw, on the floor - now that's neat !

✎

Rodrick, how would you address a Dutchman and his twin brother ?

In double Dutch, Miss !

✎

My little Ben is doing so well at school - he can speak 3 languages fluently -

Double Dutch, complete twaddle and utter gibberish !

✎

What do you get if you look at a vampire teacher through a telescope ?

A horrorscope !

Why was the teacher chased by a hen ?

It was after his wages - he said he got paid chicken feed !

How does a maths teacher remove hard wax from his ears ?

He works it out with his pencil !

You've been playing with that blotting paper the whole lesson -

You obviously find it very absorbing !

Blenkinsop, name five things that contain milk!

Yogurt, cheese, and 3 cows!

✎

My Brian is very quick at picking up music - they always send for him when they want to move the school piano!

✎

Now, for your Art homework I want you to draw a self portrait!

Does it matter who it's a portrait of, Miss?

✎

How did people react when electricity was first discovered?

They got a nasty shock!

✎

How did people react when gas was first used to heat homes?

Most people were happy, but one or two people were a bit sniffy about it!

Why is Blenkinsop at the hospital today ?

Because we had to change lessons yesterday !

How on earth can that injure anyone ?

Well, we usually have cookery - but it was changed to chemistry - and Blenkinsop always licks the spoon !

What is an alkali ?

When a drunk tells you something that isn't true !

Why did the music teacher tell his pupil to beat it ?

He was teaching him to play the bass drum !

✎

What sort of music makes a teacher take his shoes off ?

Soul music !

✎

What is the first thing teachers at the Frankenstein school do every morning ?

They go into assembly !

✎

What do you call a satellite that takes secret pictures ?

An unidentified spying object !

✎

Is the maths teacher in a good mood today ?

I wouldn't count on it !

How do you make the school loudmouth into the football team coach?

Easy, just pull out his teeth and put 11 seats in his mouth!

Did you hear about the ex maths teacher who worked on the stock exchange?

He was divided about whether to buy additional shares or take away his profits!

What class did the new robot teacher get on his first day?

He got all the nuts!

How does the robot teacher get out of the school at home time ?

He makes a bolt for it !

✎

What does the robot teacher's mum do for a living ?

She's a washer woman !

✎

How can you tell when a robot teacher is going mad ?

He goes screwy !

✎

Please French teacher,

Listen to me,

I don't know the French,

But I really need a Oui !

One in three people are stupid - so have a good look at two of your classmates.

If they seem OK then it's probably you!

I always come out in spots when I'm doing a maths exam!

Sounds like a bad case of decimals!

I sprained my ankle and had to miss games for 2 weeks!

Lucky you! Our sports teacher never accepts a lame excuse for missing games!

The school dinners here are untouched by human hand - there's a gorilla in the kitchen!

Our school dinners are full of iron - which is probably why they are so difficult to chew!

Our school kitchens are spotlessly clean -
which is why the food always tastes of soap !

I couldn't do my homework last night because my pen ran out, and I'm not allowed to go out of the house after dark !

Blenkinsop, what is the covering of a tree trunk called ?

Don't know, Sir !

Bark, Blenkinsop, Bark !

Woof, woof !

It's a good job your name is Mark -

Because you certainly don't seem able to get any in your exams !

Did you hear about the Spanish teacher who broke his leg, but was back at work 2 hours later ?

He made a maracas recovery !

✎

When did early people start wearing clothes ?

In the Iron Age !

✎

Sir, what would I have to write to get 3 'A' levels ?

Someone else's name at the top of your exam paper !

✎

Why did 1920s gangsters in America carry musical instrument cases ?

Because they committed robbery with violins !

✎

Can anyone tell me which is the longest night of the year ?

Yes, Miss, a fortnight !

What happens to children at magic school who misbehave?

They are ex - spelled!

✎

Mr Blenkinsop, I really think your daughter needs an encyclopaedia for school!

Why can't she walk like all her friends?

✎

Smith - why weren't you here at 8.45 this morning?

Because I was held up by that sign outside - it says 'stop children crossing'!

We're doing Byron in English class !

What was he famous for ?

I think he invented the ball point pen !

✎

Turn on the TV quick and you'll be able to see our school photograph !

Why, are they doing a programme about your school ?

No, it's Crimewatch !

✎

If we do the 10 times table, 10 times, how many times will we have done it ?

Is it a trick question ?

✎

Where do skinny teachers train ?

Puny - versity !

Where do crazy teachers train ?

Loony - versity !

Where do alien teachers train ?

Moony - versity !

Where do music teachers train ?

Tuney - versity !

Did you hear about the school cleaner who married a history teacher ?

He was brushing up some old dates and he swept her off her feet !

✎

Joe - how can you work out the age of a tree monkey ?

Cut it in half and count the rings ?

✎

You had better behave in Mr Simkins music class or you'll find yourself in treble !

✎

Good morning class - said the vampire English teacher -

-today we will learn the alphabat !

✎

The teachers have been working flat out in the staffroom, marking exam papers !

Really - I thought they were asleep as usual !

How can a school cook also be a history teacher ?

Easy - if they know more than anyone else about ancient grease !

What qualifications do I need to be a pantomime horse ?

Three neigh levels !

Smith - how do you feel about H G Wells ?

No, idea, Sir, we get all our water from a tap !

FOR SALE - MUSIC TEACHER RETIRING

One piano complete with stool, sheet music, and earplugs !

✎

Why did Catherine of Aragon marry Henry VIII ?

She was told she needed a ruler to help her with her maths exam !

✎

Blenkinsop - why haven't you learned your times table ?

Because we get the Guardian, Miss !

✎

Where would I find Offa's Dyke ?

I think you should be asking Offa that question, Miss, not me !

✎

Do you think my son has what it takes to be a pilot ?

Well - he certainly spends plenty of time with his head in the clouds !

What happens to old maths teachers ?

They are taken away !

What happens to old music teachers ?

They send in a note !

What happens to old history teachers ?

They reach their best before date !

What happens to old french teachers ?

One day they realise that un ouef is enough !

Does your father still help you with your homework ?

No, Miss, I can get it wrong all on my own now !

✎

Why does this class keep shouting Miss, Miss, Miss when you know very well that your teacher is a married woman ?

Because she keeps dodging the stuff we throw at her !

✎

Well, son, how did you find your geography exam ?

With a map and compass, how else !

✎

Why is the history teacher all dressed up in a suit and tie ?

No idea - maybe he has an important date !

✎

Smith - if I gave you £5 a week for the next 6 months what would you have ?

An insane teacher !

Apple crumble - my favourite !

Well, it was apple pie until the cook dropped it on the floor and the crust shattered !

Why did the vampire hate school on Tuesday ?

Because that was the day they had stake for school dinners !

Today is flying saucer day in school dinners -

because we get unidentified frying objects !

A SCHOOLTEACHER'S FAVOURITE THINGS...

Book The Caine Mutiny !

Film Rain Man (because then they cancel games !)

Actor Michael Caine !

Saying Absence makes the heart grow fonder !

✎

Did you hear about the science teacher who was always playing tricks on people ?

He was a real particle joker !

✎

Did you hear about the geography teacher who mapped out his career ?

Or the archaeology teacher whose job was in ruins ?

Or maybe the french teacher who decided one day that un oeuf was un oeuf !

Head - You'll start on a salary of £15,000 and then go up to £20,000 in six months time.

Teacher - In that case I think I would like to start in six months time!

✎

Blenkinsop, I think you need glasses!

What makes you think that, Sir?

You're facing the wrong way!

✎

Lewis - what do you get if you drop a piano down a mineshaft?

A flat minor!

✎

Did you hear about the school head who gave a pupil some lines for the first time in his career -

it was head line news!

Blenkinsop, how many times have I told you not to eat sweets in class ?

Six, Miss !

Rather more than six I think, young man !

Yes, but that's as far as I can count !

If you want to test the theory about a link between television and violence - try telling your maths teacher that you sat and watched television all night instead of doing your homework !

Sir, have you ever hunted bear ?

No, Blenkinsop, but I've been fishing in a pair of swimming trunks !

✎

Does anyone know why the Romans built straight roads?

Yes, Sir, because they didn't have steering wheels on their chariots !

✎

In your Christmas exam you wrote that there were 25 letters in the alphabet. What were you thinking of ?

Noel !

✎

What do they have for lunch at monster school ?

Human Beans on toast !

✎

What do you call an assistant headteacher who thinks he's a cowboy ?

The Deputy Head !

When does Mother Nature need a pencil?

When the Winter nights start drawing in!

✎

Where does the vampire teacher's girlfriend work?

In the class necks to his!

Do your pupils miss you ?

No, that's why I've got this bruise on my forehead !

✎

What musical instrument does the school cat play ?

A Mouse organ !

✎

What sort of insect plays music ?

A Humbug !

✎

Why are school singing classes like someone locked out of his house ?

Because neither of them can find the right key !

✎

To get a job as head of geography you need abroad knowledge of the subject !

SCHOOL LIBRARY - NEW BOOKS

The Haunted House
by
Hugo First !

The Broken Window
by
Eva Brickatit !

The Filthy Chinese Farmhouse
by
Who Flung Dung !

The Hungry Man
by
Edna Breakfast !

Why did the teacher leave his job ?

He was head hunted !

✎

Blenkinsop, why are you looking in lost property ?

My granny moved house last week and I can't remember where she lives now !

✎

Surely you can remember what happened in 1066 ?

It's alright for you, sir, you were there !

Sarah. I think your father has been helping you with your homework!

No, Miss, he did it all by himself!

✎

Today we are going to look for the lowest common denominator...

Haven't they found that yet, my dad says they were looking for that when he was at school!

✎

Blenkinsop - you deserve a hundred lines for this homework!

Ah, but it wouldn't be fair on the rest of the class if I always got what I deserved would it, sir!

Parent - Do you think my son will make a good Arctic explorer ?

Teacher - I would think so, most of his marks are below zero !

✎

Teacher - You should have been here at 9 o'clock this morning !

Pupil - Why, did something happen ?

✎

Please don't talk while you are doing your exam !

It's alright, miss, we're not doing the exam - just talking !

Science teacher - Name two liquids that don't freeze...

Mary - Coffee and tea !

History teacher - Who shot King Harold ?

Blenkinsop - My mum told me never to tell tales !

Geography teacher - Where is Hadrian's wall ?

Blenkinsop - Where he left it !

Why are maths teachers no good at gardening?

Because everything they plant grows square roots!

✎

Did you hear about the maths teacher whose mistakes started to multiply?

They took him away in the end!

✎

Did you hear about the two history teachers who met on television?

They were on Blind Date!

✎

Did you hear about the stupid P.E. teacher?

He was a physical jerk!

Susie, How do you make a milk shake ?

Take it to a scary film, Miss !

Blenkinsop, do you understand how important punctuation is ?

Yes, Miss, I always make sure I get to school on time !

Mark, how did Moses cut the sea in half ?

With a sea-saw !

✎

Wendy, when do you like school the best ?

During the school holidays, Sir !

✎

What do skeleton teachers say at the start of the lesson ?

As there is nobody here we can start !

Brian, what is water ?

A colourless liquid which turns black when I put my hands in it !

✎

You, boy, which part of a fish weighs the most ?

The scales, sir !

✎

What do Atilla the Hun and Winnie the Pooh have in common ?

The !

Smith, name me someone who has been
round the globe ?

Terminator, Miss !

Who on earth is Terminator ?

My goldfish !

✎

Watson, shouldn't you wash your hands before you
start your piano lesson ?

No, Miss, I only play on the black notes !

✎

Carol, what is the difference between a
policeman and a soldier ?

You can't dip a policeman into your boiled egg, Sir !

Now, Roger, if a half filled barrel of beer fell on someone, how badly hurt would they be ?

Not at all if it was light ale, Miss !

✎

Why are you putting in those ear plugs ?

I've got to teach form 4B tennis, and they always make such a racket !

Now, can anyone tell me what Egyptian Kings were buried with ?

Yes, Miss, they were buried with their Nammaforrs !

What is a Nammaforr ?

Knocking nails in !

Blenkinsop, how can you prove that the Earth is round ?

I didn't say it was, Sir !

What do you call a teacher swearing ?

A Sir - Cuss !

What did you think of your first day at school Joe ?

First ? You mean I have to go back again ?

What is the difference between frogspawn and school pudding?

Frogspawn was once warm!

How can you tell if a teacher is in a good mood?

Let me know if you ever find out!

Why are you always late for school?

It's not my fault, you always ring the bell before I get here!

Why did the teacher make you take the chicken out of the classroom?

He said he didn't want anyone to hear fowl language in his lesson!

Howard, which is the largest sea ?

The Galax-sea !

✎

What is a bunsen burner used for ?

Setting fire to bunsens, Miss ?

✎

Sir, can we do some work on the Iron Age today ?

Well, I'm not certain, I'm a bit rusty on that period of history !

Smith, How would you hire a horse?

Put a brick under each leg?

Why did Cyclops have to retire from teaching?

He only had one pupil!

Why is your homework late, Bloggs?

Sorry, Miss, my Dad is a slow writer!

Did you hear about the teacher who went to a mind reader?

She gave him his money back!

Blenkinsop, how do you get rid of varnish ?

Just take out the 'R', Miss !

✎

Smith, where do fish sleep ?

On a waterbed !

✎

Harry, what does it mean if I say
'Guten Morgen Herr Dresser' ?

It means you've gone for a haircut !

Sally, what musical instrument do Spanish fishermen play ?

Cast - a - nets !

Bill, which is heavier, a full moon or a half moon ?

A half moon, because a full moon is lighter !

Mary, how did you find the questions in your English exam ?

Oh, I found the questions easily enough, it's the answers I couldn't find !

Geoff, why are you eating with a knife ?

Because my fork leaks !

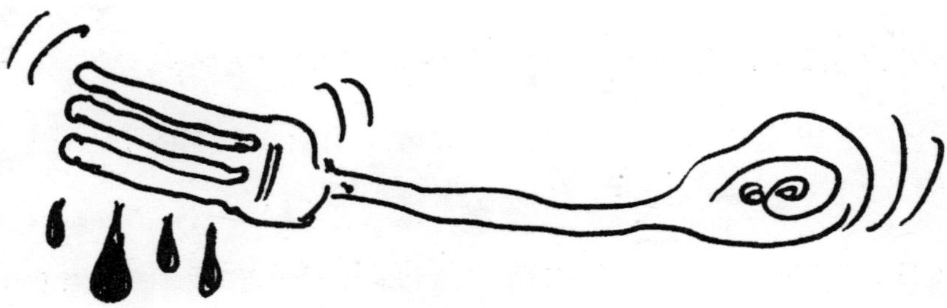

Who invented fractions ?

Henry the eighth !

Ten cats were at the cinema. One walked out. How many were left ?

None - they were all copycats !

Wally, what is a dumb waiter ?

Someone who gets all the orders mixed up, Sir !

Sue, describe crude oil for me !

Well, Sir, it is black and sticky and it floats on the surface of water shouting 'knickers' !

Joe, how many seconds are there in a year ?

Twelve, Miss, January 2nd, February 2nd, March 2nd, April 2nd....

Flora, what is the most important tool we use in mathematics ?

Multi - pliers !

Fred, where do most spiders live ?

Crawley !

Did you hear about the two history teachers who got married?

They liked to sit at home talking about old times!

✎

Where did the metalwork teacher meet his wife?

In a bar!

✎

What happened after the wheel was first invented?

It caused a revolution!

✎

Robert, why do doctors and nurses wear masks in the operating theatre?

So no-one will know who did it if they make a mistake!

✎

How do archaeologists get into locked tombs?

Do they use a skeleton key, Miss?

I've just got a place in the school football team – the games teacher says I'm the main drawback!

✎

Steven, why did Henry the eighth have so many wives?

He liked to chop and change, Miss?

✎

Why did the very first chips not taste very nice?

Because they were fried in ancient Greece!

Sarah, where would you find a gorilla ?

In a kitchen ?

✎

Jane, what do you know about the Dead Sea ?

I didn't even know it had been poorly, Sir !

✎

William, what is a fungi ?

A mushroom that likes having a good time ?

✎

'John can't come to school today, because he has a cold.'

'Who am I speaking to ?'

'My father.'

Harry, spell mouse trap...

C. A. T. !

✎

Where do vampire teachers train ?

Teacher Draining College !

✎

Billy, what is a wombat ?

It's what you use to play Wom, Miss !

✎

Carol, can you give me a sentence with deliberate in it ?

'My dad bought a new settee and tomorrow they are going to deliberate to our house !'

What do you call the teacher who organises all the exams?

Mark!

Blenkinsop, I do wish you would pay a little attention!

I'm paying as little as I can, Sir!

Fred, how do fleas get from one animal to another ?

They itch hike !

✎

Gloria, did you write this poem all by yourself ?

Yes, Miss !

Well, well, and I thought Shakespeare was a man !

✎

John, what is the longest word in the English dictionary ?

Elastic !

How do you work that out ?

It stretches !

✎

James, give me a sentence with the word fascinate in it !

Fatty Perkins' coat has ten buttons, but he can only fascinate of them !

Howard, if I had 12 sausages in one hand, and 15 sausages in the other, how many sausages would I have altogether ?

No idea, Miss, I'm a vegetarian !

✎

Freda will make a good astronomer when she leaves school, as she is very good at staring into space for hours on end !

✎

What makes you think that my son, Martin, is always playing truant ?

Martin ? There's no Martin in this school !

What do you call a man who keeps on talking when no-one is listening ?

Sir !

✎

I hope I don't catch you cheating in the maths exam !

So do I, Miss !

✎

Fred, what food do giraffes eat ?

Neck - tarines !

✎

Mary, why have you brought that fish into school ?

Because we will be practising scales in the music lesson !

✎

Jim, why did Robin Hood steal from the rich ?

Because the poor didn't have anything worth stealing !

Florence, where were most English Kings
and Queens crowned ?

On the head !

✎

Robert, why have you been suspended from school ?

Because the boy next to me was smoking !

But if he was smoking, why were you suspended ?

Because I was the one who set fire to him !

✎

Ian, when was the Forth bridge constructed ?

After the first three had all fallen down ?

✎

Graham, what is a crane ?

A bird that can lift really heavy weights !

Philip, why do you always have two plates of food for school dinner ?

It's important to have a balanced diet, Miss !

✎

Mandy, do you have to come to school chewing gum ?

No, Sir, I can stay at home and chew it if your prefer !

Teacher: Steven, what's a computer byte?

Steven: I didn't even know they had teeth!

Where were traitors beheaded?

Just above the shoulders!

Graham, what are net profits?

What fishermen have left after paying the crew?

William, how do you make a Mexican chilli?

Take him to the South Pole, Miss!

Mum: Do you say a little prayer before you eat your school dinner ?

Son: Good heavens no – the food isn't that bad !

✎

George, you have had a very undistinguished career at this school – have you ever been first in anything ?

Only the lunch queue, Miss !

✎

Why is the school cheese on toast hairy ?

Because the cook dropped it on the floor then wiped it on her jumper !

How can bats fly without bumping into anything ?

They use their wing mirrors !

✎

Sarah, give me a sentence with the word illegal in it !

My dad took me to the bird hospital the other day and we saw a sick sparrow and an illegal !

✎

William, how fast does light travel ?

I don't know, Sir, it's already arrived by the time I wake up !

What do you give a sick bird?

Tweetment!

✎

How many maths teachers can you get in an empty Mini?

Just one - after that it isn't empty any more!

✎

Miriam, what is the hottest planet in our solar system?

Mer - Curry!

✎

Time to get up and go to school!

I don't want to go! Everyone hates me and I get bullied!

But you have to go - you're the headteacher!

✎

Fred: Our teacher left last week and we all chipped in to buy her a bottle of toilet water. It cost £15!

Jane: Wow, I would have given you a whole bucket of water from my toilet for 50 pence!

Your teacher says you're disgusting and not fit to live with pigs!

What did you say?

I stuck up for you. I said you are!

✎

Teacher: Millie, why do you say that Moses wore a wig?

Millie: Because sometimes he was seen with Aaron, and sometimes without!

Pupil - Those eggs look a bit past their best !

School Cook - Don't blame me, I only laid the tables !

✎

What do you call an American cartoonist ?

Yankee Doodle !

✎

Blenkinsop, you could be in the school football team, if it weren't for two things !

What are they, Sir ?

Your feet !

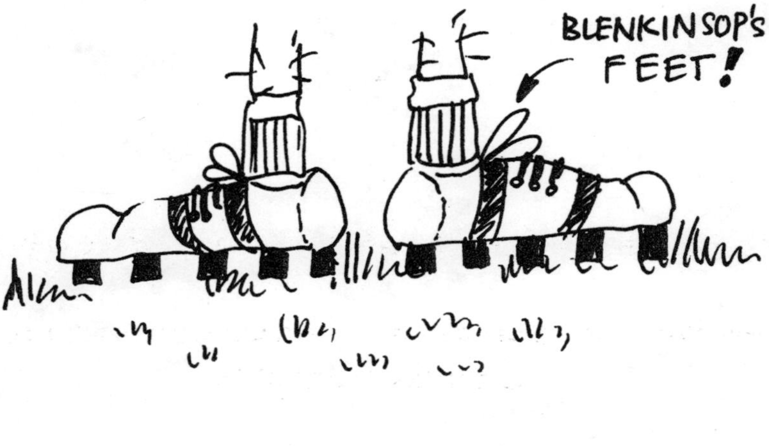

In South America, cowboys chase cattle on horseback !

WOW ! I didn't know cows could ride at all !

Who was the fastest runner of all time ?

Adam, because he was first in the human race !

My dad baked some cakes, and said I have to give one to my teacher !

Gee ! I never realised just how much he must hate your teacher !

Blenkinsop - Why do birds fly South in the Winter ?

Because it is too far to walk !

What is a snake's favourite subject ?

Hissss-tory !

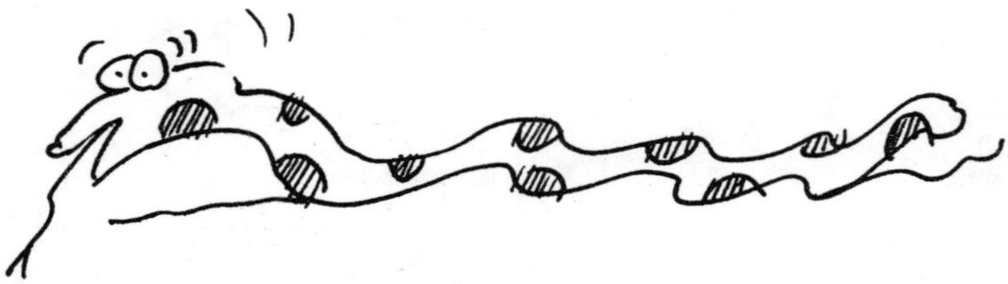

I told my dad I needed an encyclopedia for school !

What did he say ?

He said I could go on the bus like everyone else !

Head - You start on £20,000 a year, but go on to £24,000 after the first year.

Teacher - Oh ! Well, I'll come back in a year and start work then !

What does an elf do after school?

Gnome work!

✎

You have to be a really good whistler to use the school toilets here!

Why is that?

The locks are all broken!

✎

If I cut a potato in two, I have two halves.
If I cut a potato in four, I have four quarters.
What do I have if I cut a potato in sixteen?

Chips!

How did knights make chain mail?

From steel wool?

Why did the flea get thrown out of school?

He just wasn't up to scratch!

Why was the glow worm sad?

Because her children weren't very bright!

In this examination you will be allowed
15 minutes for each question!

Crikey, they sound like long questions!

What did the music teacher need a ladder for?

Reaching the top notes!

Your son will be a good printer's assistant!

What makes you say that?

He's exactly the right type!

Did you have any problems with your French on your school trip to Paris?

No, but the French certainly did!

✎

Terry - how do you join the Police Force?

Handcuff them together?

✎

John, name one use of Beech wood!

Making deck chairs?

What is easy to get into, but
difficult to get out of ?

Trouble !

My mum says the school beef pie is good for you
because it is full of iron !

That explains why it's so tough then !

What was the blackbird doing in the school library ?

Looking for bookworms !

Mary, what do you think a pair of crocodile shoes would cost ?

That would depend on the size of your crocodile's feet Miss !

✎

Fred, I told you to write 100 lines because your hand-writing is so bad, but you have only done 75 !

Sorry Miss, but my maths is just as bad as my handwriting !

Jim, what is 'won't' short for ?

Will not, Miss !

Very good. What is 'don't' short for ?

Er...Donut Miss ?

✎

Harry, how would you fix a short circuit ?

Add some more wire to make it longer, Sir ?

Where do dim witches go ?

Spelling classes !

✎

Well, Geoff, did you get a good position in the maths test yesterday ?

Yes, Sir, I was in front of a radiator, and next to the smartest person in the class !

✎

What is the most important letter to a stick insect ?

The letter 'T' - without it he would be a sick insect !

Do you know a boy called Jim Wibley ?

Yes, he sleeps next to me in Geography !

✎

Michael, can you name two inventions that have helped mankind to get up in the world ?

... Yes, Miss, the stepladder and the alarm clock !

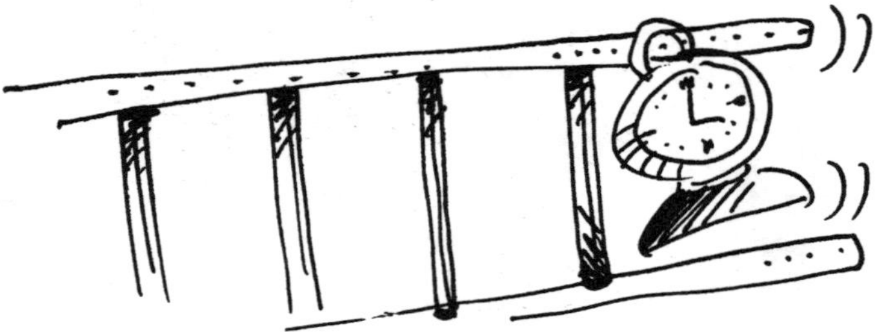

✎

What do you call it when the Headteacher doesn't tell the truth about nits in his hair ?

Head Lice !

✎

How many teachers work at your new school Samantha ?

About half of them !

Why was the teacher's head eleven inches long ?

Because if it was twelve inches it would be a foot !

✎

What was Richard the Third's middle name ?

The !

✎

You shouldn't play those notes on the piano !

Why not ?

You'll get into treble if you do !

Caroline, how many days of the week start with the letter 'T'?

Four; Tuesday,
Thursday,
Today and
Tomorrow!

✎

The School Notice Board

Violin for sale - really cheap - no strings attached!

✎

Dog free to good home - eats anything.
Loves children!

Why did the school orchestra have such awful manners ?

Because it didn't know how to conduct itself !

✎

What comes out of a teacher's wallet at 100 miles an hour ?

Stirling Moth !

✎

Table for sale, by Mr Wibley with wooden legs !

On the school field trip a crab bit my toe!

Which one?

I don't know, all crabs look the same to me!

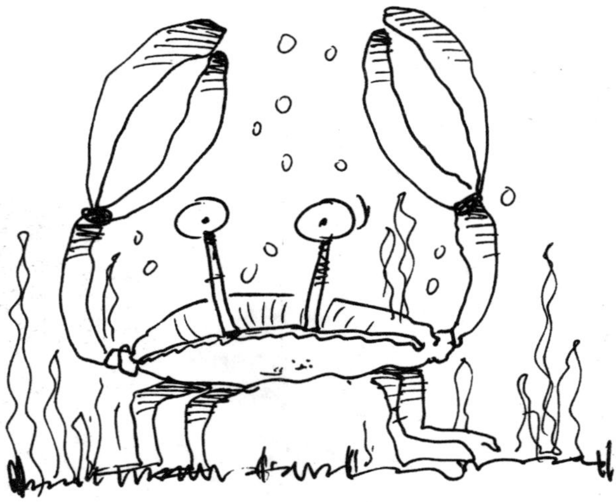

KNOCK, KNOCK...

Knock, Knock !
Who's there ?
Justin
Justin who ?
Justin time to let me in !

✎

Knock, Knock !
Who's there ?
Anna
Anna who ?
Anna noying habit of yours - locking the door like this !

✎

Knock, Knock !
Who's there ?
Josie
Josie who ?
Josie anyone else out here ?

✎

Knock, Knock !
Who's there ?
Paula
Paula who ?
Paula door open and you'll see !

Knock, Knock!
Who's there?
Annette
Annette who?
Annette Curtain!

✎

Knock, Knock!
Who's there?
Angus
Angus who?
Angus me coat up and put the kettle on!

Knock, Knock!
Who's there?
Elvis
Elvis who?
Elvis is a turnup for the books!

✎

Knock, Knock!
Who's there?
Alma
Alma who?
Alma time seems to be spent on this doorstep!

✎

Knock, Knock!
Who's there?
Zeke
Zeke who?
Zeke and you will find out!

✎

Knock, Knock!
Who's there?
Phil
Phil who?
Phil this cup with sugar would you, I've run out!

Knock, Knock!
Who's there?
Homer
Homer who?
Homer goodness, I've come to the wrong house!

Knock, Knock!
Who's there?
Alex
Alex who?
Alex the way you've done the garden!

Knock, Knock!
Who's there?
Chas
Chas who?
Chas pass the key through the letter box and I'll open the door myself!

Knock, Knock!
Who's there?
Mo
Mo who?
Mo than you'll ever know!

✎

Knock, Knock!
Who's there?
Matt
Matt who?
Matt as well settle down, looks like I'm in for a long wait!

✎

Knock, Knock!
Who's there?
Dana
Dana who?
Dana nice day out here, hurry up and let me in!

✎

Knock, Knock!
Who's there?
A. Lister
A. Lister who?
A. Lister good reasons why you should open the door!

Knock, Knock!
Who's there?
Zeb
Zeb who?
Zeb better be a good reason for keeping me waiting out here!

✎

Knock, Knock!
Who's there?
Greta
Greta who?
Greta friend like that again, and you'll end up with none at all!

✎

Knock, Knock!
Who's there?
Paul
Paul who?
Paul the door open for goodness sake!

✎

Knock, Knock!
Who's there?
Will
Will who?
Will I have to wait much longer?

Knock, Knock!
Who's there?
Woody
Woody who?
Woody open the door if we asked him nicely?

✎

Knock, Knock!
Who's there?
Kline
Kline who?
Kline of you to invite me round!

✎

Knock, Knock!
Who's there?
Polly
Polly who?
Polly door handle again, I think it's just stiff!

Knock, Knock!
Who's there?
Keith
Keith who?
Keith your hands where I can see them!

✎

Knock, Knock!
Who's there?
Imogen
Imogen who?
Imogen you were out here...

✎

Knock, Knock!
Who's there?
India
India who?
India is some of my stuff, and I've come to collect it!

✎

Knock, Knock!
Who's there?
Kat
Kat who?
Kat you again?

Knock, Knock!
Who's there?
Al Gore
Al Gore who?
Al Gore to the window so you can see me!

Knock, Knock!
Who's there?
Alvin
Alvin who?
Alvin your heart - just you vait and see!

Knock, Knock!
Who's there?
Tom
Tom who?
Tom to the window and have a look!

Knock, Knock!
Who's there?
Candy
Candy who?
Candy owner of this big red car come and move it off my drive!

Knock, Knock!
Who's there?
Alfie
Alfie who?
Alfie good to see you again!

Knock, Knock!
Who's there?
Kim
Kim who?
Kim just too late to see you!

Knock, Knock!
Who's there?
Adair
Adair who?
Adair you to guess!

Knock, Knock!
Who's there?
Chuck
Chuck who?
Chuck the key under the door and I'll let myself in!

✎

Knock, Knock!
Who's there?
Khan
Khan who?
Khan you give me a lift to school?

✎

Knock, Knock!
Who's there?
Mavis
Mavis who?
Mavis be the last time you keep me waiting!

✎

Knock, Knock!
Who's there?
Darren
Darren who?
Darren nother excuse to keep me out here!

Knock, Knock!
Who's there?
Luke
Luke who?
Luke through the letterflap and you'll see!

✎

Knock, Knock!
Who's there?
Colin
Colin who?
Colin in for a chat!

✎

Knock, Knock!
Who's there?
Wendy
Wendy who?
Wendy you want me to call round again?

Knock, Knock!
Who's there?
Tori
Tori who?
Tori - I got the wrong address!

Knock, Knock!
Who's there?
Trudy
Trudy who?
Trudy my word I've come to collect you!

Knock, Knock!
Who's there?
Trish
Trish who?
Bless you!

Knock, Knock!
Who's there?
Cameron
Cameron who?
Cameron say that!

Knock, Knock!
Who's there?
I Know Kung fu
I Know Kung fu who?
I'd better not upset you then!

Knock, Knock!
Who's there?
Cohen
Cohen who?
Cohen to knock just once more, then I'm going away!

Knock, Knock!
Who's there?
Kent
Kent who?
Kent you stop asking questions and open the door!

Knock, Knock!
Who's there?
Alan
Alan who?
Alan 'nounce myself once you've opened the door!!

Knock, Knock!
Who's there?
Penny
Penny who?
Penny for the guy mister?!

Knock, Knock!
Who's there?
Postman
Postman who?
Just the postman with your letters - you're thinking of Doctor Who!

Knock, Knock!
Who's there?
Ahmed
Ahmed who?
Ahmed a big mistake coming here didn't I?!

Knock, Knock!
Who's there?
Ginger
Ginger who?
Ginger hear the doorbell?

Knock, Knock!
Who's there?
Courtney
Courtney who?
Courtney door, can you open it and let me loose?

Knock, Knock!
Who's there?
Isabell
Isabell who?
Isabell not working?

Knock, Knock!
Who's there?
Eeny Minnie
Eeny Minnie who?
Eeny Minnie Miny Mo!

✎

Knock, Knock!
Who's there?
Guess Simon
Guess Simon who?
Guess Simon the wrong doorstep!

✎

Knock, Knock!
Who's there?
Wendy
Wendy who?
Wendy red, red robin comes bob, bob bobbin' along, along...

✎

Knock, Knock!
Who's there?
Wendy
Wendy who?
Wendy come to collect the rent, I'm off!

Knock, Knock!
Who's there?
Amos
Amos who?
Amos quito is chasing me - please let me in!

✎

Knock, Knock!
Who's there?
Arnie
Arnie who?
Arnie ever going to let me in ?!

✎

Knock, Knock!
Who's there?
Ken
Ken who?
Ken you come out to play?

✎

Knock, Knock!
Who's there?
Sid
Sid who?
Sid you'd be ready to go at three - what's gone wrong!

Knock, Knock !
Who's there ?
Seymour
Seymour who ?
Seymour of me by opening the door !

Knock, Knock !
Who's there ?
Sid
Sid who ?
Sid down and I'll explain !

Knock, Knock !
Who's there ?
Charlie
Charlie who ?
Charlie you know the sound of my voice by now !

Knock, Knock !
Who's there ?
Hedda
Hedda who ?
Hedda nough of this - I'm off !

Knock, Knock!
Who's there?
Ivan
Ivan who?
Ivan idea you're going to keep me waiting out here!

Knock, Knock!
Who's there?
Gin
Gin who?
Gin know how cold it is out here!

Knock, Knock!
Who's there?
Farmer
Farmer who?
Farmer distance your house looks much bigger!

Knock, Knock !
Who's there ?
Linda
Linda who ?
Linda hand to get this heavy suitcase up the steps !

✎

Knock, Knock !
Who's there ?
Tex
Tex who ?
Tex you ages to open the door !

✎

Knock, Knock !
Who's there ?
Hardy
Hardy who ?
Hardy har, fooled you !

✎

Knock, Knock !
Who's there ?
Yul
Yul who ?
Yul soon see !

Knock, Knock!
Who's there?
Courtney
Courtney who?
Courtney good football matches lately!

Knock, Knock!
Who's there?
Mary
Mary who?
Mary Christmas, ho, ho, ho!

Knock, Knock!
Who's there?
Carla
Carla who?
Carla taxi, I'm leaving!

Knock, Knock!
Who's there?
Giraffe
Giraffe who?
Giraffe to ask me that stupid question?

Knock, Knock!
Who's there?
Paul
Paul who?
Paul the door from your side - it's a bit stiff!

Knock, Knock!
Who's there?
Ringo
Ringo who?
Ringo, ringo roses...!

Knock, Knock!
Who's there?
Mike
Mike who?
Mike your mind up!

Knock, Knock!
Who's there?
Spock
Spock who?
Spock the difference between me and my twin brother!

Knock, Knock!
Who's there?
Teacher
Teacher who?
Teacher self for a few days, I'm off on my hols!

Knock, Knock!
Who's there?
Tessa
Tessa who?
Tessa long time for you to open the door!

✎

Knock, Knock!
Who's there?
Carl
Carl who?
Carl round to my house and I won't keep you waiting!

✎

Knock, Knock!
Who's there?
You
You who?
Hello!

✎

Knock, Knock!
Who's there?
Simon
Simon who?
Simon every occasion - you always make me wait!

Knock, Knock!
Who's there?
Princess
Princess who?
Princess not to come round here any more !

✎

Knock, Knock!
Who's there?
Morgan
Morgan who?
Morgan you could ever imagine!

✎

Knock, Knock!
Who's there?
Jacqueline
Jacqueline who?
Jacqueline Hyde !!

Knock, Knock!
Who's there?
Callista
Callista who?
Callista warm reception I was expecting!

✎

Knock, Knock!
Who's there?
Teresa
Teresa who?
Teresa jolly good fellow !

✎

Knock, Knock!
Who's there?
Mouse
Mouse who?
Mouse get a key of my own!

✎

Knock, Knock!
Who's there?
Batman
Batman who?
You mean there's more than one ?!

Knock, Knock!
Who's there?
Donna
Donna who?
Donna knock once more then I'm going home!

Knock, Knock!
Who's there?
Egbert
Egbert who?
Egbert no bacon!

Knock, Knock!
Who's there?
Misty
Misty who?
Misty door bell again!

Knock, Knock!
Who's there?
Lester
Lester who?
Lester worry about!

Knock, Knock!
Who's there?
Just Paul
Just Paul who?
Just Pauling your leg - it's Steve really!

✎

Knock, Knock!
Who's there?
Fitz
Fitz who?
**Fitz not too much trouble -
can you please open the door!**

✎

Knock, Knock!
Who's there?
Major
Major who?
Major mind up to open the door yet?

✎

Knock, Knock!
Who's there?
Mandy
Mandy who?
Mandy lifeboats!

Knock, Knock!
Who's there?
Belle
Belle who?
Belle don't work, so I'm having to knock!

✎

Knock, Knock!
Who's there?
Alex
Alex who?
Alex to knock on doors and run away!

Knock, Knock !
Who's there ?
Vance
Vance who ?
Vance more I knock on your door in the dead of night !

Knock, Knock !
Who's there ?
Yootha
Yootha who ?
Yootha person with the second hand cooker for sale ?

Knock, Knock !
Who's there ?
Ozzie
Ozzie who ?
Ozzie you still have the same front door you did the last time I called !

Knock, Knock !
Who's there ?
Chester
Chester who ?
Chester minute - I'm in the wrong street !

Knock, Knock!
Who's there?
Carl
Carl who?
Carl this a friendly greeting – 'cos I don't!

Knock, Knock!
Who's there?
Mustapha
Mustapha who?
Mustapha good reason to keep me waiting!

Knock, Knock!
Who's there?
Willy
Willy who?
Willy hurry up and let me in!

Knock, Knock!
Who's there?
Posh
Posh who?
Posh the door open and you'll see !

✎

Knock, Knock!
Who's there?
Baby
Baby who?
Baby I shouldn't hab come round wiv dis cold!

✎

Knock, Knock!
Who's there?
Fred
Fred who?
Fred you'll have to let me in!

✎

Knock, Knock!
Who's there?
Russell
Russell who?
**Russell up a nice hot cup of tea -
it's freezing out here!**

Knock, Knock!
Who's there?
Homer
Homer who?
Homer goodness - I can't remember myself !

Knock, Knock!
Who's there?
Bart
Bart who?
Bart time you opened this door!

Knock, Knock!
Who's there?
Denise
Denise who?
Denise are cold - let me in!

Knock, Knock !
Who's there ?
May
May who ?
May I come in ?

✎

Knock, Knock !
Who's there ?
Lass
Lass who ?
How long have you been a cowboy ?

✎

Knock, Knock !
Who's there ?
Doctor
Doctor who ?
No, Doctor Smith - you sent for me because you have a cold !

✎

Knock, Knock !
Who's there ?
Norbut
Norbut who ?
Norbut a lad !

Knock, Knock!
Who's there?
Giselle
Giselle who?
Giselle flowers in there?

✎

Knock, Knock!
Who's there?
Will
Will who?
Will wait out here until you let us in!

✎

Knock, Knock!
Who's there?
Jaffa
Jaffa who?
Jaffa keep me waiting?

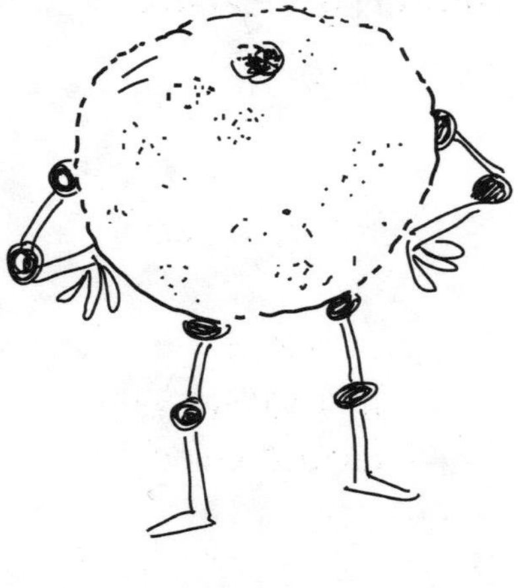

Knock, Knock !
Who's there ?
Posy
Posy who ?
Posy open the door and find out ?

✎

Knock, Knock !
Who's there ?
Terminator
Terminator who ?
Terminator sandwiches early, so she sent me to get some more !

✎

Knock, Knock !
Who's there ?
Yul
Yul who ?
Yuletide greetings neighbour !

✎

Knock, Knock !
Who's there ?
Walter
Walter who ?
Walter strange thing to ask !

Knock, Knock!
Who's there?
Wade
Wade who?
Wade a minute I'll just check!

Knock, Knock!
Who's there?
Jerome
Jerome who?
Jerome at last!

Knock, Knock!
Who's there?
Karl
Karl who?
Karl again another day!

Knock, Knock !
Who's there ?
Vince
Vince who ?
Vince some time since I saw you last !

Knock, Knock !
Who's there ?
Donna
Donna who ?
Donna expect you to remember me !

Knock, Knock !
Who's there ?
Red
Red who ?
Red your letters, you can have them back now !

Knock, Knock !
Who's there ?
Pearce
Pearce who ?
Pearce this balloon with a pin !

Knock, Knock !
Who's there ?
Jools
Jools who ?
Jools like these should be worth a lot of money !

Knock, Knock !
Who's there ?
Whoo ooo oooo ooo
Whoo ooo oooo ooo who ?
Ah, good, this is the ghosts club !

Knock, Knock !
Who's there ?
Fletch
Fletch who ?
Fletch a bucket of water, your house is on fire !

Knock, Knock !
Who's there ?
Icing
Icing who ?
Icing carols - you give me money !

Knock, Knock!
Who's there?
Chris
Chris who?
Chris packets make a lot of noise in the cinema!

Knock, Knock!
Who's there?
Jethro
Jethro who?
Jethro this at me?

Knock, Knock!
Who's there?
Vicar
Vicar who?
Vicar might have caught something nasty!

✎

Knock, Knock!
Who's there?
Dan
Dan who?
Dan just stand there - let me in!

✎

Knock, Knock!
Who's there?
Lefty
Lefty who?
Lefty home on your own again!

✎

Knock, Knock!
Who's there?
Yul
Yul who?
Yul see when you open the door!

Knock, Knock!
Who's there?
Arthur
Arthur who?
Arthur minute and I'll show you my identification!

Knock, Knock!
Who's there?
Mickey
Mickey who?
Mickey fell down the drain, can you give me a lift?

Knock, Knock!
Who's there?
Mayor
Mayor who?
Mayor come in?

Knock, Knock!
Who's there?
Butcher
Butcher who?
Butcher said I could come and visit you!

Knock, Knock!
Who's there?
Greengrocer
Greengrocer who?
Greengrocer rushes oh!

✎

Knock, Knock!
Who's there?
Al
Al who?
Al huff and I'll puff and blow your house down!

✎

Knock, Knock!
Who's there?
Howard
Howard who?
Howard you know if you won't even open the door?

Knock, Knock !
Who's there ?
Elvis
Elvis who ?
Elvis is a complete waste of time. I'm off !

Knock, Knock !
Who's there ?
Olly
Olly who ?
Olly need is love !

Knock, Knock!
Who's there?
Colin
Colin who?
Colin round to see you!

Knock, Knock!
Who's there?
Lucinda
Lucinda who?
Lucinda sky with diamonds...!

Knock, Knock!
Who's there?
Jester
Jester who?
Jester day, all my troubles seemed so far away...!

Knock, Knock!
Who's there?
Our Tell
Our Tell who?
Our Tell you what I want, what I really really want...!

Knock, Knock !
Who's there ?
Honor Claire
Honor Claire who ?
Honor Claire day, you can see forever...!

✎

Knock, Knock !
Who's there ?
Carrie
Carrie who ?
Carrie your bags to the airport for a fiver ?

✎

Knock, Knock !
Who's there ?
Avon
Avon who ?
Avon to trink your blood !

✎

Knock, Knock !
Who's there ?
Otto
Otto who ?
Ottold you not two seconds ago !

Knock, Knock!
Who's there?
Carter
Carter who?
Carter stray dog - is it yours?

✎

Knock, Knock!
Who's there?
Woody
Woody who?
Woody lend me a tenner till payday?

✎

Knock, Knock!
Who's there?
Joanna
Joanna who?
Joanna have a guess?

✎

Knock, Knock!
Who's there?
Wallace
Wallace who?
Wallace is a fine how do you do...!

SPOOKY STUFF

Should baby monsters eat humans on an empty stomach ?

No, they should eat them on a plate like everyone else !

How do monsters write letters?

With fountain men !

Why do monster mums and dads tell their children to eat cabbage ?

Because they want them to have a healthy green complexion !

Why did the ghost get the job ?

Because he was clearly superior !

Did you hear about the giant monster who took a hump-back in a plastic box to work with him ?

It was his packed hunch !

What did the monster get when he fell through a window ?

A pane !

✎

What do they sing in the vampire version of Abba ?

Fang you for the music !

✎

Why did the zombie go to the chemist ?

He wanted something to help stop his coffin !

✎

What is the first thing you should put into a haunted house ?

Someone else !

✎

What do they employ in monster hospitals ?

A skeleton staff !

Baby Monster - When I grow up I want to drive a tank!

Mummy Monster - Well, I certainly won't stand in your way!

✎

Why was the monster called porridge?

Because he was grey and thick!

✎

What should you do after shaking hands with a monster?

Count your fingers!

✎

What is a monster's favourite game?

Squash!

✎

Did you hear about the zombie who was having a party - he didn't know how many people would be coming - it would depend on who he could dig up!

What did the blacksmith do when he saw Frankenstein's neck ?

He made a bolt for it !

How did the fruit bats go into Noah's Ark ?

In pears !

Did the computerised monster have any brothers ?

No, but he had hundreds of tran - sisters !

How do slimy monsters fight?

They just slug it out!

What posh school do cannibal monsters go to?

Eton!

Did you hear about the vampire who got his big break on television?

He got a job hosting the National Clottery!

How did you know I was a ghost?

Oh, I can see right through you!

✎

When a vampire drinks too much, what does he get?

A Fangover!

✎

Why do vampires go to lots of pop concerts?

They love being in fang clubs!

✎

What did King Tut-Ankh-Amun hate most of all?

Having to go shopping with his *mummy*!

✎

Why was the *mummy* covered in gold and silver shiny bandages with big bows?

It was his Christmas wrapping!

Did you hear about the mummy who wanted to be a rock star?

He started his own rock bandage!

What do ghostly policemen do?

They haunt down criminals!

What sort of monsters work in graveyards?

A skeleton staff!

Did you hear about the werewolf who dropped his trousers?

Well – it was a full moon!

How do you scare vampires ?

Ask if they would like a little garlic with their steak !

✎

How does a vampire lock his coffin ?

With skeleton keys !

✎

Did you hear about the overweight cannibal from Sweden ?

He was always eating swedes between meals !

✎

How do monsters eat their dinner ?

They wolf it down !

✎

Why was the vampires bank account always in the red ?

Because it was in a blood bank !

Why did one skeleton tell the other one off ?

Because he had been telling fibulas !

✎

What sort of monster lives in your hanky ?

A bogeyman !

✎

What sort of monster drinks tinned blood ?

A Canpire !

✎

What do monsters eat for a light meal ?

Light bulbs !

✎

What does a monster call knights in armour ?

Tinned food !

Hurry up, said the father skeleton to his son, or you'll be late for the skull bus !

Why does the monster shop at the sewage works ?

He likes convenience food !

What is the first thing a monster eats in a restaurant ?

The waiter !

What do vampires eat for lunch ?

Fangers and mash !

What did the monster say when he threw a human into a pit of werewolves ?

Looks like you're going to the dogs !

✎

Why is the tribe of Bolog now extinct ?

Because monsters used to eat lots of spagetti with Bolog knees !

✎

Where did the vampire go on his holiday in China ?

Fang - Hi !

✎

Why are vampires good at treating people with coughs and colds ?

Because they can clear your throat in seconds !

✎

Why do vampires like joggers ?

They adore fast food !

Why is monster coffee so noisy ?

Because they like scream in it !

✎

What is the shortest and nastiest party game that monsters know ?

Swallow the leader !

✎

Why do monsters make good fashion models ?

Because no matter what they are wearing they always look so ghoul !

What do you call a pair of ghostly glasses ?

Spectre - calls !

What do you take to a vampire party ?

The girl necks door !

How did the ghostly teacher make sure his pupils had learned what he had written on the blackboard ?

He went through it again !

What do you call a James Bond monster
who is only interested in gold!

Ghoul finger!

✎

How do two monsters decide who
owns something?

They fright each other for it!

✎

How do vampires try out a new blood group?

They suck it and see!

✎

How do vampires get clean?

In a blood bath!

✎

What do you call a vampire with no teeth?

Pointless!

What noise do baby witches make when they are playing with toy cars ?

Broom, Broom !

✎

What is a ghosts favourite film ?

The Deer Haunter !

✎

Why was the stone monster always short of money ?

He was always hard up !

✎

What do you call a kind, helpful monster who likes flowers and butterflies ?

A Failure !

✎

What fictional character are werewolves afraid of ?

Long John Silver !

Who do vampires invite to their weddings ?

All their blood relatives !

✎

Why do ghosts never feel guilty ?

They have a clear conscience !

✎

What do you call a vampire that you can dip into your tea ?

Count Dunkula !

Why do vampires never invite trolls to their dinner parties?

They can't stand all that goblin!

✎

What tennis players do monsters like to eat?

Bjorn on the cob!

✎

What did the vampire do when someone accused him of drinking blood?

He didn't bat an eyelid!

✎

Why should you never invite monsters to a housewarming party?

Because they bring flame throwers!

✎

What does a monster send you on your birthday if he doesn't like you?

A Scratchcard!

Why should you never play cricket with Dracula?

Because he might let his vampire bat!

I see Dracula has a new job -
he's a cashier in a blood bank!

You know that a barking vampire dog never bites....

....but when it stops barking, you better run!

How do vampires show affection for each other ?

They bat their eyelids !

✎

What do you call a hairy monster that's lost ?

A where-am-I wolf !

✎

What do you call an escaped hairy monster ?

A where's-he-gone wolf !

✎

What is Frankenstein's worst nightmare ?

Being nude in a room full of people - without a stitch on !

✎

What do you get if you put a monster on your roof ?

A bite on the tiles !

When Mr Dracula put on his coat one evening his wife asked if he was going to the pub with his friends.

No, dear, he replied. Just popping out for a bite !

What is a ghost's car called ?

Squeals on wheels !

What does Dracula drink ?

De-coffinated - coffee !

What does Dracula have fitted to the front of his car ?

Head vamps !

✎

Which monster ate the three bears ?

Ghouldilocks !

✎

What did Dracula say when someone said his teeth were ugly ?

I'll fang you not to say that !

✎

What sort of view do you get from the top of a pyramid ?

As Pharoah the eye can see !

✎

What would you be if your daddy was a mummy and you were musical ?

A wrap singer !

What is a monster's favourite TV soap ?

Beastenders !

✎

A vampire started acting very strangely, and a passer-by asked if he was going mad - the vampire replied that he was perfectly sane, but just felt a little batty !

✎

Did you hear about the monster who fell asleep in an empty coffin ?

It was a grave mistake !

✎

My husband always looks a mess whenever there's a full moon -

he's really going to the dogs !

✎

Did you hear about the vampire burglar who was caught red handed ?

They caught him fang to rights !

What pets does Dracula own?

A Blood Hound and A Ghoul Fish!

Why do vampires have a steady nerve?

They are as ghoul as cucumbers!

Why do zombies always look so tired?

They are dead on their feet!

Why did Dracula advertise for a housekeeper ?

He wanted some new blood in the house !

✎

Did you hear about the monster who went into a restaurant and ordered crocodile and chips ?

He was in a hurry so he shouted, "and make it snappy !"

✎

If you're good at writing, Dracula has a job for you...

...he's looking for someone to answer his fang mail,

...and take on the job as his crypt writer !

✎

How do you get a message to a deep sea monster ?

Drop him a line !

✎

Why is the sea monster wet ?

Because the seaweed !

How do you know what a deep sea monster looks like ?

He's the one with the wavy hair !

How do you know if a monster fancies you ?

He'll roll his eyes at you !

And what should you do if that happens ?

Roll them back before someone steps on them !

In the monster version of the story of Snow White, what are the seven dwarves called ?

Snacks !

Why do vampires avoid arguments ?

They hate to get cross !

✎

What did the doctor say to the vampire with acid indigestion ?

"Stop drinking acid !"

✎

The monster went to his doctor and complained of a split personality.

Do sit down, the doctor said, and begin by telling me which one of you is paying !

✎

"I think I need new glasses," said the short sighted monster.

"You certainly do," replied the dentist !

✎

Who do you telephone to rent a Dracula costume ?

Vamp - hire !

How do you know if you had a drunken vampire at your party?

There are fang marks on the ketchup bottle!

What did Frankenstein do when the monster's head kept falling off?

He made a bolt for it!

What do you get if you cross a vampire with a robot?

Something new fangled!

Oh, red eyed vampire in the night,

you nearly gave my heart a fright.

All black and shiny, glistening red,

from pongy toes to slithery head.

If you had hoped to drink my blood,

and hoped that it would do you good,

I think you made a big mistake,

'cos I'd just been out for a steak!

✎

Why did Dracula want to keep his baby teeth for all eternity?

Because a fang of beauty is a joy forever!

Which window cleaners do vampires use ?

The one in pane - sylvania !

✎

Why do monsters like to stand in a ring ?

They love being part of a vicious circle !

✎

What do you call a ghostly teddy bear ?

Winnie the OOOoooooOooooohhHHhhhhh !

Why did the vampire go to the blood donor centre ?

To get lunch !

✎

What do you call a Welsh ghost ?

Dai !

✎

What do you call a tough Welsh ghost that stars in an action movie ?

Dai Hard !

✎

Why did the England cricket team consult a vampire ?

They wanted to put some bite into the opening bats !

How do vampires start a duel?

They stand Drac to Drac!

When do ghosts wear red jackets and ride horses?

When they go out fox haunting!

Why are owls so brave at night?

Because they don't give a hoot for ghosts, monsters or vampires!

What did the old vampire say when he broke his teeth ?

Fangs for the memory !

✎

Why do vampires holiday at the seaside ?

They love to be near the ghostguard stations !

✎

What is the ghostly Prime Minister called ?

Tony Scare !

✎

What do you call a dentist who really likes vampires ?

An extractor fan !

What do you call a futuristic android who comes back in time to plant seeds ?

Germinator !

✎

And what do you call his twin brother ?

Germinator II !

✎

What do you call the ghost of the handkerchief ?

The Bogie man !

✎

What sort of wolf can you wear ?

A wear wolf !

✎

What sort of wolf delivers Christmas presents ?

Santa Claws !

What do you call a lazy skeleton ?

Bone Idle !

What do you call a ghostly would-be Scottish King ?

Boney Prince Charlie !

Why do ghosts catch cold so easily ?

They get chilled to the marrow !

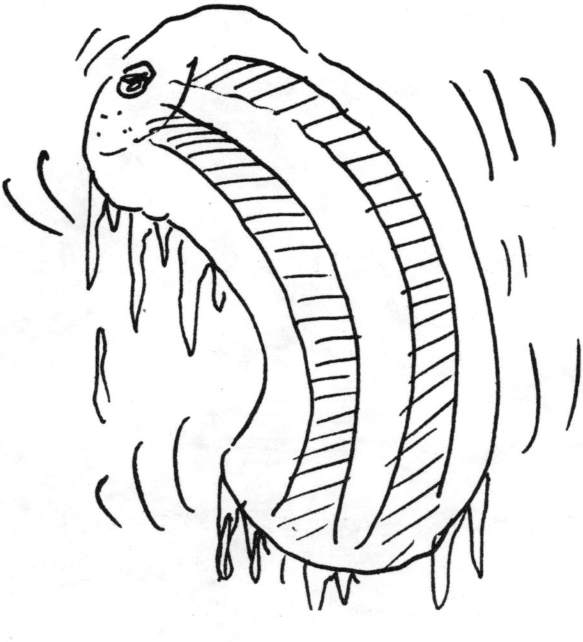

What do you call a scary, boney creature that staggers around making strange wailing noises ?

A supermodel making a record !

✎

Why are skeletons no good at telling lies ?

Because you can see right through them !

✎

What should you say when a vampire gives you a present ?

Fang you very much !

Why don't vampires like modern things?

Because they hate anything new fangled!

✎

What do monsters like to pour on their Sunday dinner?

Grave-y!

✎

What do you call a ghostly haircut with long curly strands of hair?

Deadlocks!

✎

What do ghosts like with their food?

A little whine!

What film is about a scary train robber ?

Ghost Buster !

✎

Where do ghosts live ?

In flats !

✎

Where do vampires like to go for their holidays ?

The Dead Sea !

✎

Why did the two vampire bats get married ?

Because they were heels over heads in love !

What did the pirate get when he smashed a skeleton up in a fight ?

A skull and very cross bones !

Where do skeletons cook their meals ?

In a skullery !

What do you call a young skeleton in a cap and uniform ?

A skullboy !

Why did the skeleton fall into a hole ?

It was a grave mistake !

✎

What villain does the spooky 007 fight ?

Ghoulfinger !

✎

Why are hyenas always falling out ?

They always have a bone to pick with each other !

✎

Who delivers Christmas presents to vampires ?

Sack-ula !

What vampire can you wear to protect you from the rain?

Mac - ula!

✎

What is the fairy tale about a girl who falls in love with a really ugly loaf of bread?

Beauty and the yeast!

✎

When they got married, what sort of children did they have?

Bun-shees!

✎

Why did Goldilocks go to Egypt?

She wanted to see the mummy bear!

AND, SPEAKING OF MUMMIES...

Mummy, mummy, what is a vampire?

Be quiet and eat your soup before it clots!

✎

Mummy, mummy, what is a werewolf?

Be quiet and comb your face!

✎

Mummy, mummy
I don't like my
uncle Fred!

Well, just leave him on the side of your plate and eat the chips!

✎

Mummy, mummy I don't want to go to America!

Be quiet and keep swimming!

Mummy, mummy I'm just going out for a quick bite to eat!

OK, but make sure you're back in your coffin before daybreak!

✎

What did the monster say when the vampire asked for his daughter's hand in marriage?

OK, we'll eat the rest!

✎

Why do some ghosts paint themselves with black and white stripes?

So they can frighten people on Pelican crossings!

OR

So they can play for Boocastle United!

What should you wear when you go out for a drink with a vampire?

A metal collar!

What do you call a young woman who hunts vampires?

A Miss Stake!

What do the police call it when they watch a vampire's house?

A stake out!

What does the monster Tarzan eat for tea?

Snake and pygmy pie with chips!

What did the ghostly show jumper always score?

A clear round!

What did the young ghost call his mum and dad?

His trans-parents!

Why don't you have to worry what you say to the werewolf computer engineer?

His bark is worse than his byte!

What sort of jokes do werewolves like best ?

Howlers !

✎

What happens when a werewolf meets a vampire ?

He doesn't turn a hair !

✎

Why wasn't the werewolf allowed to get off the lunar spaceship ?

Because the moon was full !

✎

Why did the werewolf start going to the gym ?

Because he liked the changing rooms !

What did the train driver say to the werewolf ?

Keep the change !

Why did the werewolf steal underwear when the moon was full ?

Because his doctor told him a change was as good as a vest !

What sort of news do werewolves fear ?

Silver bulletins !

Why did the shy werewolf hide in a cupboard every full moon?

Because he didn't like anyone to see him changing!

✎

What form of self defence do werewolves use?

Coyote!

✎

How do mummies knock on doors?

They wrap as hard as they can!

✎

Why was the mummy done up in brightly coloured sparkly paper?

He was gift-wrapped!

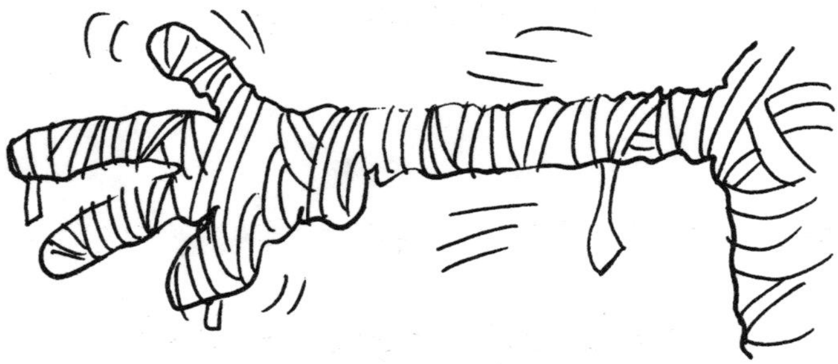

What does it say on the mummy's garage entrance ?

Toot, and come in !

What do mummies use to fasten things together ?

A Hammer and Niles !

What do children in Egypt call their parents ?

Mummy and Daddy of course !

Why was the Egyptian Prince worried?

Because his mummy and daddy were both mummies!

What do mummies shout when they are on a sinking boat?

A bandage ship!

What do mummies do to relax?

They just unwind a little!

Why was the mummy's leg stiff?

Because someone had been winding him up!

What are the scariest dinosaurs ?

Terror dactyls !

✎

Why are mummies good at keeping secrets ?

They can keep things under wraps for centuries !

✎

What did the monster say when it saw someone going past on a mountain bike ?

Ah! Meals on wheels !

✎

What did the ghost of the owl say ?

Too-wit too-woooooooooooo....

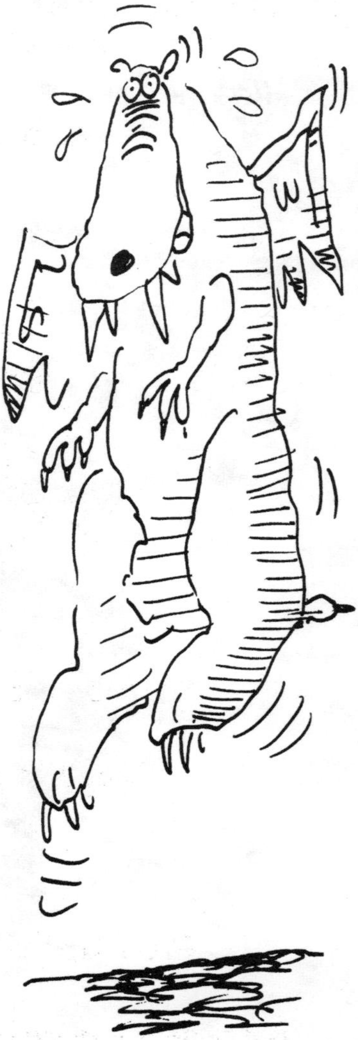

Why is Godzilla sitting on a friend like leaving home ?

Because you end up with a flat mate !

✎

Who was the winner of the headless horse race ?

No-one, they all finished neck and neck !

✎

What did the President of the USA say to the giant ape when he won the lottery ?

Kong - ratulations !

What eats your letters when you post them ?

A ghost box !

What spook delivers your letters ?

Ghostman Pat and his skeleton cat !

Which creature saves people from drowning ?

The Ghostguard !

Why did the vampire like eating chewy sweets ?

He liked something to get his teeth into !

Why do sausages and bacon spit when they are being cooked ?

Because it's a terror frying experience !

What is the scariest thing you could find in your Christmas stocking?

The ghost of Christmas presents!

✎

Why did the vampire put tomato ketchup on his sandwiches?

He was a vegetarian!

✎

How do you grow a werewolf from a seed?

Just use plenty of fur-tiliser!

Why can you never get through to a vampire bat on the telephone ?

Because they always hang up !

✎

What football teams does Dracula support ?

Shiverpool !

Fang-chester United !

Scream Park Rangers !

✎

What football team does Frankenstein's monster support ?

Bolt - On Wanderers !

What is a werewolf's favourite film?

The Full Moonty!

✎

What lies at the bottom of the sea and shivers?

A nervous wreck!

✎

Which vampire likes playing practical jokes?

Dracu-lark!

✎

Where do vampires keep their savings?

In the ghost office!

What did Jeremy Paxman say to the werewolf team on University Challenge?

No con-furring!

✎

What pop group did the young mummies join?

A boy bandage!

✎

What would you call a mummified cat?

A first aid kit!

✎

Why was Dracula ill after biting someone on a train home from work?

He caught a commuter virus!

If hairy palms is the first sign of turning into a monster, what is the second ?

Looking for them !

How do you stop a werewolf attacking you ?

Throw a stick for it to fetch !

What was on the haunted aeroplane ?

An air ghostess and a lot of high spirits !

Why couldn't the ghost get a whisky in the pub after 11 o'clock?

Because they aren't allowed to serve spirits after closing time!

✎

Why did the witch take her small book of magic on holiday?

The doctor told her to get away for a little spell!

✎

Who was the fattest mummy ever?

Two ton Carmen!

Why couldn't the witch's victim move ?

He was spellbound !

What sort of horses do monsters ride ?

Night mares !

What do sea monsters eat ?

Fish and ships !

Why do sea monsters go to so many parties ?

They like to have a whale of a time !

Which sea monster rules the waves ?

The Cod-father !

What do baby sea monsters play with ?

Doll-fins !

What do you give a monster that feels sick ?

Plenty of room !

✎

Where do monsters sleep ?

Anywhere they want to !

✎

What do you get if a monster falls over in a car park ?

Traffic jam !

✎

What would you get if you combined a monster, a vampire, a werewolf and a ghost?

As far away as possible !

What do monsters call a crowded swimming pool ?

Soup !

✎

What do you get if you shoot a werewolf with a silver bullet ?

A very interesting rug !

✎

What do you call the ghost of a werewolf that lives at the seaside ?

A Clear - Pier - Were - Wolf !

✎

How did Frankenstein's monster escape from the police ?

He made a bolt for it !

✎

Why did Dracula visit a psychiatrist ?

He thought he was going batty !

What sort of music do vampires and ghosts like best ?

Haunted House Music !

✎

If a monster buys you a chair for your birthday should you accept it ?

Yes - but don't let him plug it in !

✎

What does a monster shout when it is scared ?

Mummy !

✎

Can you stick vampires to your window ?

Yes - they are suckers !

✎

Why did the ghost go to the bicycle shop ?

He needed some new spooks for his front wheel !

Where do ghouls live?

Bury!

What game do ghouls play?

Bury St Edmonds!

What do you call a stupid vampire?

A clot!

What sort of jobs do spooks like ?

Dead end jobs !

✎

What do ghosts do at parties ?

They have a wail of a time !

✎

Who do vampires invite to their birthday parties ?

Anybody they can dig up !

Why don't ghosts go out during the day ?

They are scared of people !

Why don't skeletons have glass eyes ?

Because they come out in conversation !

Why are vampires always cheerful ?

Because they are terrified of being cross !

What is a werewolf's favourite film ?

Claws !

What sort of voice do werewolves have ?

Husky ones !

✎

What do werewolves hate most ?

When people lead them a dog's life !

What do you get if you cross a vampire with a knight of the round table?

A Bite in shining armour!

What was Dr Frankenstein best at?

Making new friends!

What do spooks eat in the morning?

A hearty breakfast of Dreaded Wheat!

Why didn't the vampire laugh at the joke about the wooden stake?

He didn't get the point!

What do you get if you cross the Abominable Snowman and Count Dracula?

Severe frostbite!

Where do spooks go shopping?

In BOOOO-tiques!

What did the spook begin his letter with ?

Tomb it may concern....

✎

Where is the invisible man ?

No idea, I haven't seen him around for ages !

✎

What did the sign in the pyramid shop say ?

Satisfaction guaranteed or your mummy back !

Why are vampires so thin?

They eat necks to nothing!

Why did the ghoul take so long to finish his newspaper?

He wasn't very hungry!

Why did the monster eat a settee and two armchairs?

He had developed a suite tooth!

Why did the vampire bats hanging in the church belfry look exactly the same as each other ?

They were dead ringers !

✎

Why didn't the spook win the lottery ?

He didn't have a ghost of a chance !

✎

Why did the ghost of Guy Fawkes go crazy ?

It's OK, he just lost his head for a moment !

Wow - did you see that wolf ?

Where ?

No - it was just an ordinary one !

✎

What sport do monsters like best ?

Sculling !

✎

How do you know when there is a horrible monster under your bed ?

You don't - that's what makes it so very scary !

DUMBER AND DUMBER

How do you make hot cross buns?

Turn their central heating up too high!

✎

Just because your hand is 12 inches long, that doesn't mean that it's a foot!

✎

How do you confuse an idiot?

I'll tell you tomorrow!

✎

What does Tarzan eat on Saturday nights?

Fish and chimps!

✎

Did you hear about the idiot who went to a car boot sale?

He now owns six car boots!

How did the midget alien get into the police force ?

He lied about his age !

✎

What is yellow and highly dangerous ?

Shark infested custard !

✎

Why should you dial carefully if you 'phone Mr Wing in China ?

You might ring the Wong number !

✎

What's the point of custard ?

It's only blue on Wednesday !

Did you hear about the man who joined the army because he wanted to be a drill sargeant ?

They gave him a Black & Decker !

✎

What happens when a witch catches the flu ?

Everyone gets a cold spell !

✎

Did you hear where the stonemason took his girlfriend ?

To a rock concert !

✎

Did you hear where the fizzy drinks maker took his girlfriend ?

To a pop concert !

✎

What does an idiot do when he wins the round the World yacht race ?

He does a lap of honour !

What happened when the idiot made a paper plane ?

Someone hijacked it !

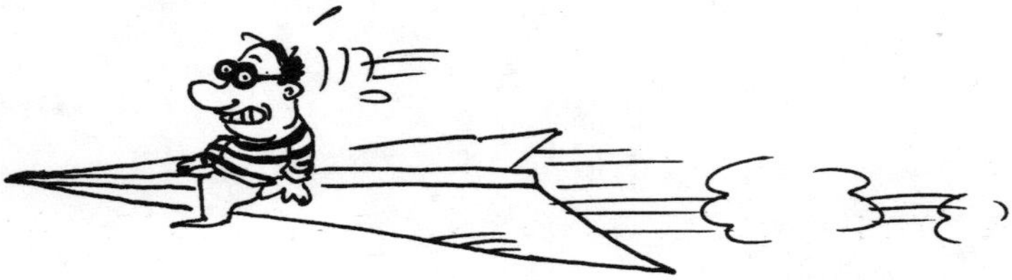

✎

My dad says that in the future all trains and buses will run on time !

Rubbish, they'll still run on petrol like they do now !

✎

Why did the idiot apply for a job as a language teacher ?

Because someone told him he spoke perfect rubbish !

✎

Waiter, can I have my lunch on the patio ?

Certainly, Sir, but most people find a plate more sensible !

Why did the monster swallow a bag full of pennies?

Because he thought the change would do him good!

Why was the trout's piano off key?

Because he couldn't find the piano tuna!

I bought myself a pocket calculator for Christmas - now I know exactly how many pockets I have!

Why did the skeleton not go to the dance?

Because he had no body to go with!

Why should you never tell secrets in a corn field ?

Because you would be surrounded by ears !

✎

Did you hear about the failed magician ?

He had one half brother and one half sister !

✎

Mmmmm ! This jam sponge cake is
lovely and warm !

**It should be, the cat's been sitting on
it all afternoon !**

✎

Why did the robot need a manicure ?

He had rusty nails !

✎

What did the werewolf say to the vampire ?

It's been so nice getting to gnaw you !

I love all my teachers,
from my head down to my belly.
I love to do my homework,
even though I miss the telly.
I love to do detention,
and I love to work real late.
I polish all the teachers shoes,
I really think they're great.
They're kind and smart and helpful,
they're delicate and gentle.
And I am - yes, you've guessed it -
very, very mental !

✎

Why couldn't the butterfly go to the dance ?

It was a moth ball !

✎

What is the difference between Sting and Walt Disney ?

Sting sings, but Walt Disney !

✎

What deep sea creature swims about in his underwear ?

The Loch Vest Monster !

A Yeti who came from Basmati,
Woke up one day feeling quite hearty.
It's those climbers I ate,
He said as he licked the plate.
I can't wait for the rescue party!

When the monster had finished eating his human, he threw the wristwatch onto a pile in the corner.

His friend asked him why he did this.

"It's too time consuming," was his fellow monster's reply!

What is the most untidy monster ever known?

The Loch Mess Monster!

What do you get if you cross a canary with a monster ?

A broken cage !

✎

What do you get if you cross a vampire with a petrol pump ?

Something that makes a hole in your car and sucks out all the petrol !

✎

Why are vampires so stupid ?

Because blood is thicker than water !

Why can you never trick the snake monster?

Because you can't pull his leg!

✎

What do you get if you cross a bird with a snake?

A feather boa constrictor!

✎

Did you hear about the sculptor's son?

He was a chip off the old block!

✎

What's the difference between margarine and a goat?

You mean you can't tell margarine from butter?

✎

Did you hear about the idiot who sold his television to raise the money to buy a video?

Or his brother, who sold his personal stereo, to get the money to buy batteries for it!

Did you hear about the triangle player who disappeared from the orchestra.....

....while they were playing the Bermuda waltz ?

✎

Did you hear about the librarian who got carried away....

....while he was reading The Invasion Of The Body Snatchers ?

✎

Waiter, waiter -there's a fly in my soup !

Sorry, madam, I didn't know you were vegetarian !

I'm never going to follow in my father's footsteps, I faint at the sight of blood!

Was your father a doctor?

No, a vampire!

✎

What do you think the invention of the safety match had on society?

I'd say it was a striking achievement!

✎

Why is a lazy schoolboy the exact opposite of Robinson Crusoe?

Because Robinson Crusoe got all his work done by Friday!

✎

You look depressed - I thought you had just started your new job as a football boot cleaner?

I have - that's why I'm depressed - I work for the centipede's eleven!

Why should you always be thankful to pigs ?

Because you should never take them for grunted !

✎

Three badly made robots were playing cards...

One threw his hand in...

Another rolled his eyes - across the floor...

The third one laughed his head off !

✎

A really bad jazz band had just finished a song.

"Any requests?" they called to the audience.

"Do you know "San Francisco ?", replied one member of the audience.

"Yes, of course," replied the band leader.

"Please go there and play."

Why did the car driver close his eyes ?

Because the traffic light was changing !

What does a ghostly builder use ?

A spirit level !

Why do vampires not like pointed stakes ?

Because they know that it's rude to point !

Two idiots were fishing in a lake, and were catching lots of fish.

They decided to come back the following weekend and catch even more fish, but they were concerned that they would not be able to find the exact spot on the lake when they next came.

Then one of them had a brilliant idea – he painted a red X on the side of the boat !

✎

Why should you never fall asleep on a train ?

Because they run over sleepers !

✎

What sort of chocolate bars do snowmen eat ?

Snowflakes !

YOU KNOW IT'S A BAD SIGN WHEN...

...you see weather men eating beans !

...travel agents close their shops and go on holiday !

...psychiatrists keep changing their minds !

...there's a fight in the chip shop, and people get battered !

...people call in a sturgeon when they get a fish bone stuck in their throat !

...a schoolboy gets locked in a cage in the classroom because he is teacher's pet !

...a maths teacher smiles !

...the plumber brings a plug for your new bath, because he thinks it is electric !

✎

What do you get if you cross a science room and a dog ?

A Lab !

Do you play the Trumpet Voluntary ?

No, my mum makes me do it !

✎

How do you know when your school bus is old ?

The seats are covered in Mammoth hide !

✎

What do they say to postmen when they make them redundant ?

"We are going to have to unsack you !"

✎

What do you call a cake you eat in the bath ?

Sponge !

✎

Remember that before you give someone a piece of your mind, you should always check that you will have enough left over for yourself !

If I should win the lottery,

Think how much fun my life would be.

No more school, or work at home,

No more school dinners that taste like foam.

No more lines, no more pain,

Just lots of telly and sweets and games.

✎

What do you call the place where all the used lottery tickets are thrown ?

The National Littery !

✎

A man of 6 feet 9 inches and another man of 4 feet 6 inches robbed a bank today....

....police are looking high and low !

✎

Why do swimming teachers like elephants ?

Because they always bring their trunks !

What do you call a man who can complete any job in 30 seconds?

Arthur Minute!

✎

What happened when two wasps had a fight?

There was a terrible BUZZZTUP!

✎

Name seven things that are grey, four legged and have a trunk!

Six elephants and a mouse going on holiday!

✎

Why did the elephant cover his trunk in suncream?

Because he didn't want to get it sunburned!

✎

How does a witch-bride get to the altar?

On a Groom Stick!

What sort of crisps do really nasty monsters eat ?

Squeeze and bunion !

Did you hear about the elephant who sued the airline ?

His trunk got caught in the X-ray machine !

Why do policemen like discos ?

They like a good steady beat !

What does a witch take on holiday ?

Her sleeping hag !

✎

Where does Dracula go in the Summer ?

A holiday vamp !

✎

What was the Chinese air force commander called ?

The Wing commander !

✎

Why is Cinderella so bad at football ?

She has a pumpkin for a coach !

✎

Why do witches go to hot countries ?

For a spell in the sun !

Did you hear about the girl who put her granny's false teeth under her pillow ?

The tooth fairy left her a counterfeit £10 note !

✎

What do you call the sea monster that dresses scruffily ?

Loch Vest !

✎

Why did the farmworker punch the man in a pub ?

Because the man was eating the ploughman's lunch !

✎

What did the doctor say to the invisible man after he had swallowed some coins ?

I can't see any change in you !

✎

What insect do you find before the sea ?

The B !

Boy - Dad, am I worth £1000 to you ?

Dad - Of course you are son !

Boy - So, taking account of the 9 greenhouse windows I just smashed I reckon you owe me about £850 !

✎

What do you dial if you want to contact the German police ?

Nein, Nein, Nein !

✎

What do monsters eat with their Christmas dinner ?

Boy sprouts !

✎

How do you cut water ?

With a sea-saw !

✎

What does a Scottish owl do ?

Hoots, mon !

A man decided to start a chicken farm.. He bought 24 chicks to get started.

A week later he bought another 24 and then another 24 the week after that.

When his friend asked how his chicken farm was coming along the man replied...

..."Not one of them has grown yet. I wonder if I'm planting them too deep ?"

What choice do you get with school custard ?

Like it or lump it !

How do you make a Swiss roll ?

Push him down an Alp !

What sweet course do solicitors like best ?

Sue - it pudding !

What do you get if you cross a vampire and an ice monster ?

Frost bite !

Teacher - I'll teach you to be clever in my class !

Pupil - At last - a lesson I'll be interested in!

Why did the deaf Italian waiter smear pasta sauce on people's ankles ?

Because he thought they asked for spagetti below the knees !

What do you get from a nudist pig?

Streaky bacon!

What did Fred Flintstone shout when he had a cold?

Yabba - Dabba - Atish - ooo!

What travels along the sea bed at 90 miles an hour?

Hondawater sea creatures!

What is the difference between electricity and lightning?

Lightning is free!

What sort of animal do you need when it's cold?

An otter!

✎

Why do my schoolfriends call me a vampire?

Don't let them worry you -
just drink your tea before it clots!

✎

A bird in the hand - is likely to poo on your wrist!

✎

Where do space monks live?

In a Moon - astry!

Where do they keep old cows ?

In a MOOOseum !

✎

What do you do if you swallow a wristwatch ?

Take a laxative to help pass the time !

✎

Why did the lemon refuse to fight the orange ?

Because it was yellow !

✎

What is always dressing ?

Mayonnaise !

✎

Knock, Knock
Who's there ?
Howard.
Howard who ?
Howard I know ?

My friend John believes in free speech -

which is why he comes round to my house to telephone people !

✎

What is a Forum ?

A two - um plus a two - um !

✎

The new doctor is so witty - he'll have you in stitches !

I hope not - I've only come to see him about my sore throat !

✎

Catacomb - hair cleaning device for cats !

✎

A load of bees were getting very hot and bothered one summer's day. The queen bee asked what the trouble was...

"Swarm" came the reply !

Did the doctor give you anything for your wind ?

Yes, he gave me this kite !

Why did the doctor write on your foot ?

He said it was a footnote !

Which Shakespeare play is about pigs ?

Hamlet !

Johnny - I despair of your spelling mistakes and poor punctuation. Where is your grammar ?

She's at home watching the telly, Miss!

What do you give a pig with a sore bottom ?

Oinkment !

✎

In the olden days, false teeth were made of wood -

- do you know what tree the wood came from ?

The Gum Tree ?

✎

What did the careful robot say ?

Look before you bleep !

✎

Teacher - Blenkinsop, what is a telescope ?

Blenkinsop - something that you can watch TV with from a long way off ?

✎

Why are dinosaurs extinct ?

Because male and female dinosaurs refused to get evolved with each other !

Why was the ghost's son asked to leave the school ?

Because he was clearly too high spirited !

How many letters in hungry horse ?

Four - M. T. G. G. !

Why was the genie in the lamp angry ?

Someone rubbed him up the wrong way !

What is yellow and white and travels at
125 miles an hour ?

A train driver's egg sandwich !

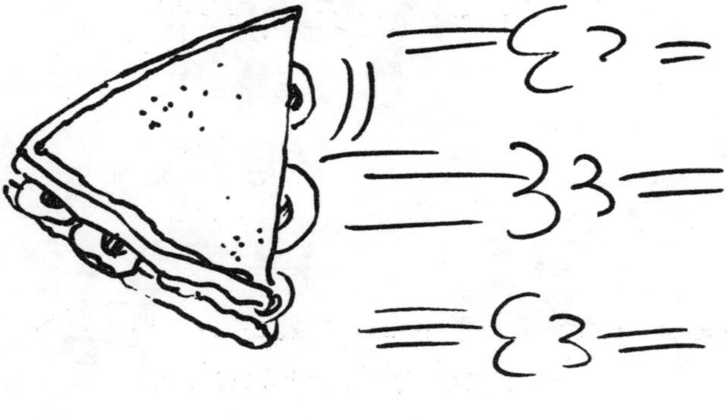

What do you get if you cross a space suit and a saddle ?

A Horse - tranaut !

✏

What is the best thing to do when a hippo sneezes ?

Get out of the way !

✏

I'd like to buy a teapot please !

Have you tried Boots ?

Yes, but it comes out through the lace holes !

Our tyres are the best that money can buy -
we skid you not !

✎

Why do football teams have to practise so much when they play against zombies ?

Because they face stiff competition !

✎

What do you get if you cross an athlete and a computer ?

A floppy discus thrower !

✎

What is red and cheeky ?

Tomato sauce !

✎

Which age did the mummies live in ?

The band - age !

Why did you decide to become a cat burglar ?

My doctor told me to take things quietly !

✎

Why do flamingoes lift one leg ?

Because if they lifted both legs they would fall over !

✎

What was the first thing that Henry VIII did on coming to the throne ?

He sat down !

✎

How many sheep does it take to make a sweater ?

Wow – I didn't even know sheep could knit !

✎

How do you make gold soup ?

Put 14 carrots in it !

Operator – get me the king of the jungle!

I'm sorry but the lion is busy right now!

✎

Why did the idiot fall asleep in a bakery?

He went there for a long loaf!

✎

What happened when the monsters ate the comedian?

It was a feast of fun!

✎

Waiter – this lemonade is cloudy!

No it isn't, sir, it's the glass that's dirty!

✎

Where were all the Kings of Italy crowned?

On the head!

My uncle spent £1000 having his family tree traced!

Crikey - I hope he didn't find out that I cut it down!

Blenkinsop, what are you doing standing out there in the rain?

Getting wet!

What do you call a man with a speedometer on his head?

Miles!

Have you been drinking your medicine
after your bath ?

No, after I have drunk the bath I just can't manage the medicine !

✎

What do you call a pimple on a Tyrannosaurus Rex ?

A Dino-sore !

✎

Our parrot lays star shaped eggs !

Wow - does it talk as well ?

It just says the one word - OUCH !

✎

Grandad, do you know how to
impersonate a frog ?

I think so, young Eric, but why ?

Because Mum says that when you
croak we'll be rich !

Doctor, my hair keeps falling out - can you give me something to keep it in?

Yes, here's a paper bag!

How does a vampire start a letter?

Tomb it may concern...

What did the inscription outside the pyramid say?

Satisfaction guaranteed - or your mummy back!

Which city is the most shocking?

Electri - city!

What fish would you find on a battery powered shoe?

An electric heel!

What kind of bow is never tied?

A Rainbow!

✎

What did the clockmaker say when he was burgled?

He's taken my valuable time!

✎

What's bright red, runs on petrol and eats cornflakes?

A motor cycle – I lied about the cornflakes!

✎

What did the fat man say when he sat down at the dinner table?

"Just think – all this food is going to waist!"

✎

What sort of books do dwarves read?

Collections of short stories!

Mary had a little lamb,
and a little pony, too.
She put the pony in a field,
and the lamb into a stew!

Humpty Dumpty sat on a wall,
Humpty Dumpty had a great fall.
All the king's horses and
all the king's men,
thought it was really funny,
and asked him to do it again!

Simple Simon
met a pieman
going to the fair.
Said Simple Simon
to the pieman,
may I taste your wares ?
Said the pieman
to Simple Simon,
I don't sell wares
but you can try one of my pies if you like !

I wandered lonely as a cloud
that floats on high o'er hill and dell.
No-one would sit next to me
'cos I had made a nasty smell !

If you can pass exams,
while all about you are failing theirs,
you're a bigger swot than I am,
Gunga Din !

**To be or not to be
that is the question,
or should I just use a pen instead!**

✎

Little Miss Muffet
sat on her tuffet
eating her favourite lunch.
A giant went by
looking up to the sky
and Little Miss Muffet went 'CRUNCH'

✎

**Little Bo-Peep
has lost all her sheep,
which is why she's down at the
job centre this morning!**

I went to the pictures tomorrow,
I got a front row seat at the back,
I bought an ice cream with a cherry on top,
I ate it and gave it them back!

The animals went in two by two,
the elephant and the kangaroo,
the lion the tiger,
the cat and the dog,
the mouse the gorilla,
the rat and the frog,
but they could only find one dinosaur,
which is why they aren't around any more!

Little Jack Horner,
sat in the corner,
eating his apple pie.
He put in his thumb,
and pulled out a plum,
and said 'that's a
funny looking apple!'

Hickory Dickory Dock,
6 mice ran up the clock.
The clock struck one,
but the other 5
got away!

Jack and Jill
went up the hill
to fetch a pail of water,
Jack fell down
and broke his crown
and Jill said
I told you you shouldn't
try and skateboard down...

A green spotted alien from Mars
liked eating motorcycles and cars.
When people cried 'shame'
he said 'It's the same...
as you lot eating Mars bars !'

At lunchtime every schoolday,
Blenkinsop (the fat),
would eat his way through everything,
except the kitchen cat.
Two plates of chips, for starters,
a pack of crisps (or three),
then on to shepherd's pie and beans,
washed down with mugs of tea.
Spaghetti Bolognese and rice,
it all went down a treat,
chicken curry, very nice,
pasties (cheese and meat).
When all the savouries had been
dispatched into his belly,
he started on the sweet menu,
(say goodbye to the jelly !)
rice pudding, jam and eccles cakes,
yogurt, custard, shortbread,
till suddenly he simply burst,
on the final slice of bread.

When Mary had a little lamb
the doctor was surprised,
but when Old Macdonald had a farm
he couldn't believe his eyes!

School, glorious school,
we love all our teachers,
our lessons are cool,
but some pupils are creatures.

I never could
quite work out why
an elephant
could never fly.
With massive ears
to flap and twitch
you'd think they'd glide
without a hitch.

YOBS AND GIRLS

My brother is the school swot !

Does he do well in exams ?

No - he just kills flies !

✎

My sister is really stupid - she bites her nails all the time !

That's not dumb - lots of people bite their nails !

Not rusty 4 inch floorboarding nails they don't !

✎

My sister was engaged to a man with a wooden leg.

Did she marry him ?

No, she broke it off !

✎

My wife said that if I didn't give up playing golf she would divorce me !

Wow - that must have been a tough decision to make ?

Yes - and I really miss her cadddying for me now !

My boyfriend is called Fog !

Is that because he is wisp like and mysterious ?

No, it's because he's wet, grey and thick !

✎

Headteacher - That is the thickest girl in the whole school !

Parent - That's my daughter you're talking about !

Headteacher - Oh, I'm terribly sorry !

Parent - You're sorry - how do you think I feel ?

✎

Our drama teacher says I've got the perfect face for radio !

My English teacher says my handwriting is so bad I could be a doctor !

✎

My science teacher says I could be an astronaut,

because I have nothing but space between my ears !

✎

Now, children, what were you before you started school ?

"Happy !"

✎

My girlfriend tried on a mud pack, and it really made her look better - but then it fell off !

✎

Did you do well in your maths test dear ?

I certainly did, Mum, I was next to a window and a radiator !

Why did the school idiot buy a sea horse?

Because he wanted to play water polo!

✎

How long is a school ome lette?

Don't be daft – it's round just like any other sort!

✎

Why did the green, slimy space monster go to see Jurassic Park?

Because he had read the book and really enjoyed it!

Three girls were exploring an old haunted house.
In one room they saw a £50 note on an old table.

The first girl went to pick it up when she heard a ghostly voice saying,
"I'm the ghost of Auntie Mabel, that £50 stays on the table !"

The second girl also tried to pick it up when the voice called out
"I'm the ghost of Betty Grable, that £50 stays on the table !"

The third girl marched straight into the room and pocketed the £50. Before the ghost could speak she called out,
"I'm the ghost of Davy Crockett, that £50 is in my pocket !"

✎

My little Geoff is a wonder child -

the teachers at his school often wonder if he'll ever learn anything !

✎

What do you do with a giant deck of playing cards ?

Big deal !

Please sir, I wouldn't get into trouble for something I haven't done would I ?

Of course not, Blenkinsop, that would be unfair !

I'm glad you said that - I haven't done my homework !

✎

If God could make a woman out of a man's rib - what did he do with all the leftovers ?

✎

My sewing teacher was away from school ill...when I asked how she was feeling she said...

"Sew, sew !"

✎

What did Snow White say as she looked through her empty photograph album ?

"Some day my prints will come !"

✎

Why did Belinda give cough medicine to the pony ?

Because Sally told her it was a little horse !

The teacher asked the class to write an essay about what they would do if they won the lottery!

Blenkinsop handed in a blank sheet of paper.

"What is the meaning of this?" she asked.

"It's what I'd do if I won the lottery - nothing!"

Melissa was playing the flute - very badly!

Her brother said, "you should be on the television playing that!"

"Wow, do you think I'm good enough?" she replied.

"No, but at least I could turn you off!"

Why do monsters have to pay twice when they go to the zoo ?

Once to get in and once to get out !

✎

Of course your shoes hurt - you've put them on the wrong feet !

But they're the only feet I have !

✎

What did one salt pot maker say to the other salt pot maker when they first met ?

Shake !

✎

What did the alien say to the petrol pump ?

"Take your finger out of your ear when I'm talking to you !"

✎

I just love school dinners, but they make my belly so fat !

Have you tried to diet ?

No - what colour would be best ?

Why did the crocodile buy his son a camera?

Because he was always snapping!

Doctor, doctor, my sister thinks she's a lift!

You had better tell her to come in and see me!

I can't - she doesn't stop at this floor!

I met my first girlfriend at a printmaker's disco -

But it didn't last, she wasn't the right type for me!

What would you do if a jellyfish stung you ?

I'd break every bone in its body !

✎

Why did the schoolboy bite the dentist ?

Because he got on his nerves !

✎

If I were a schoolboy,
All over again,
I'd work really hard,
And never get the cane.
I'd pass exams,
Just like that,
I'd even remember,
To wear my cap.
Then one day,
If my dream came true,
I'd be a teacher,
Just like you !
I hope you like my poem,
I don't want to make you sad, but....
It was written by a boy,
Who is totally MAD !

My cookery teacher is a chip off the old block!

Why was the boy who had cake upset?

Because it was stomach cake!

How did the schoolgirl swim at over 60 mph?

She swam over a waterfall!

Why was Cinderalla rubbish at games ?

Because her coach was a pumpkin !

✎

What were the 16 schoolboys playing in the telephone box ?

Squash !

✎

What were Tarzan's last words ?

Who moved that vine !

✎

What work does Mrs Claus give Santa Claus to do in the garden ?

Ho Ho Hoeing !

✎

What did they call the cowboy after someone stole all his cash ?

Skint Eastwood !

An apple a day keeps the doctor away -

An onion a day keeps everyone else away !

✎

How did the schoolboy stop the elephant from smelling ?

He tied a knot in its trunk !

✎

How should you show your appreciation to a vampire ?

With a fang-you letter !

✎

Blenkinsop - you are good at picking up music -
go and move the piano from the music room
to the assembly hall !

✎

This homework looks a though it has been written by your father ?

Well it would do, I borrowed his pen !

How do you help Frankenstein's monster ?

Give him a hand when he needs it !

✎

Millie - what does it mean when the barometer falls ?

It means my dad is useless at knocking nails into the wall !

What happened to the Scottish schoolboy who washed his kilt ?

Now he can't do a fling with it !

✎

Blenkinsop - I think you need glasses !

But I'm already wearing glasses !

In that case I need glasses !

✎

How do you wake chickens in the morning ?

With an alarm cluck !

✎

What is a maybe ?

A bee born in May !

✎

Which famous knight never won a single battle ?

Sir Endor !

Why are mummies good at writing exams ?

Because they keep everything under wraps !

✎

What has 22 legs and 2 wings but can't fly ?

The school football team !

✎

How do you keep a fool waiting...?

I'll tell you tomorrow !

✎

What is the name of that teacher with soil on his head ?

Pete !

✎

Sir, this chair isn't very comfortable !

Of course it is, Blenkinsop, it's sat in !

What do you call a man with a tree growing out of his head?

Ed - Wood!

How do you stop a head cold going to your chest?

Easy - tie a knot in your neck!

Why shouldn't you try to swim on a full stomach?

Because it's easier to swim on a full swimming pool!

What creature sticks to the bottom of sheep ships?

Baaa - nacles!

How do you know if your little brother is turning into a fridge?

See if a little light comes on whenever he opens his mouth!

✎

What is the coldest part of the North Pole?

An explorer's nose!

✎

What do computer operators eat for lunch?

Chips!

Why is that man standing in the sink ?

He's a tap dancer !

✎

Where do rabbits learn to fly ?

In the Hare Force !

✎

How did the witch know she was getting better ?

Because the doctor let her get out of bed for a spell !

What did the witch call her baby daughter ?

Wanda !

How do witch children listen to stories ?

Spellbound !

Which witch went to Ipswich ?
The rich witch called little Mitch,
with the light switch for the soccer pitch,
who twitched and fell in a ditch;
that witch went to Ipswich -
and never came home !

What would you find in a rabbit's library?

Bucks!

✎

Where do fish like going for their holidays?

Finland!

✎

What did the overweight ballet dancer perform?

The dance of the sugar plump fairy!

Why is it easy to swindle a sheep ?

Because it is so easy to pull the wool over its eyes !

✎

What do elves eat at parties ?

Fairy Cakes !

✎

What do you get if you cross a brain surgeon and a herd of cows ?

Cow-operation !

✎

Why did the carpenter go to the doctor ?

He had a saw hand !

What is the only true cure for dandruff ?

Baldness !

✎

What should you buy if your hair falls out ?

A good vacuum cleaner !

✎

A man went to see his doctor with a brick buried in his head. What was he suffering from ?

Falling arches !

Why did the doctor operate on the man who swallowed a pink biro ?

He had a cute-pen-inside-is !

Nurse - why are you putting Mr Smith's left leg in plaster, it's his right leg that's broken ?

It's OK, I'm new so I'm practising on the left one first to make sure I do it properly!

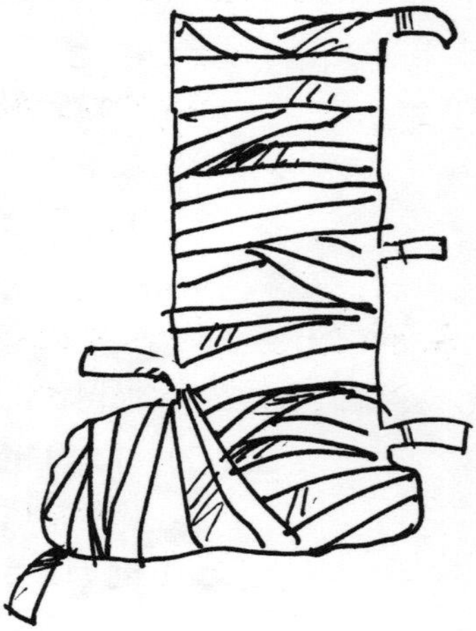

What sort of fish would you find in a bird cage ?

A Perch !

What sort of fish would you find in a shoe ?

An Eel !

What sort of dance do fish do at parties ?

The Conga !

Where did the dog breeder keep his savings ?

In bark-lays bank !

Did you hear about the bungee jumper who shot up and down for 3 hours before they could bring him under control ?

He had a yo-yo in his pocket !

What do you call a cowboy who helps out in a school?

The Deputy Head!

What do you call the teacher in the school who gives out forms that you have to fill in?

The Form Teacher!

Did you hear about the dog who was arrested?

He didn't pay a barking ticket!

Where did the rich cat live?

In a mews cottage!

✎

What position did the witch play in the football team?

Sweeper!

✎

What position did the pile of wood play in the football team?

De-fence!

Why couldn't the slow boxer get a drink at the party ?

Because everyone beat him to the punch !

Why was the archaeologist upset ?

His job was in ruins !

Why was the butcher worried ?

His job was at steak !

Why did the teacher have to turn the lights on?

Because his pupils were so dim!

Why did the French farmer only keep the one chicken?

Because in France one egg is un oeuf!

What did the farmer say when all his cows charged him at once?

I'm on the horns of a dilemma here!

What sort of snake will tell on you?

A grass snake!

Why did the doll blush?

Because she saw the Teddy Bear!

POINTLESS INVENTIONS...

Camouflage for stick insects!

Disposable rubbish bags!

Colour radio!

Invisible traffic lights!

Plastic tea bags!

Waterproof soap!

Fireproof petrol!

What sort of ring is always square?

A boxing ring!

✎

What sort of queue is always straight?

A snooker cue!

✎

What sort of net is useless for catching fish?

A football net!

Why do people leave letters at the football ground?

They want to catch the last goal-post!

✎

I've got a terrible fat belly!

Have you tried to diet?

Yes, but whatever colour I use it still looks fat!

✎

What do you call a frog that helps children safely across the street?

The green cross toad!

✎

Did you hear about the posh chef with an attitude problem?

He had a french fried potato on his shoulder!

Why do golfers carry a spare sock?

Because they might get a hole in one!

✎

A rather dim gardener from Leeds,
once swallowed a packet of seeds.
In just a few weeks,
his ears turned to leeks,
and his hair was a tangle of weeds!

✎

I once met a man from Hong Kong,
who'd been jogging for twenty years long.
He was terribly sweaty,
- he looked like a yeti,
and his feet had a terrible pong!

What book do you buy to teach children how to fight ?

A scrapbook !

✎

What sort of animals make the best TV presenters ?

Gnus - readers !

✎

What sort of animal is best at getting up in the morning ?

A LLama clock !

I hear you've just invented gunpowder ?

Yes, I was using some candles to light my laboratory and it came to me in a flash !

How is your other invention coming along - you know, the matches ?

Oh ! They've been a striking success !

Why did the doctor take his nose to pieces ?

He wanted to see what made it run !

Why is it dangerous to tell jokes to Humpty Dumpty ?

He might crack up !

Blenkinsop - stop acting the fool - I'm in charge of this class, not *you*!

Why do pens get sent to prison?

To do long sentences!

What was the parrot doing in prison?

It was a jail-bird!

What is the name of the detective who sings quietly to himself while solving crimes ?

Sherlock Hums !

✎

Why did the farmer feed his pigs sugar and vinegar ?

He wanted sweet and sour pork !

✎

What do you call the Scottish dentist ?

Phil McCavity !

✎

Why is the soil in my garden always dry ?

Because you have leeks !

What kind of rose
has a bark ?

A dog rose !

✎

What did the little
boy say when he
wanted his big
brother to give him
back his building
bricks ?

Lego !

✎

Why are you called
Postman Pat ?

**Because I have to
deliver post to all
the farms !**

✎

Which two words
in the English
language have the
most letters ?

Post Office !

How do you start a jelly baby race?

Ready - Set - Go!

What sort of music was invented by fish?

Sole music!

What gets smaller the more you put in it?

A hole in the ground!

Waiter, why is there a dead fly in my soup ?

Well, you surely don't expect to get a live one at these prices !

✎

What happened to the man who stole a lorry load of eggs ?

He gave himself up - he said he only did it for a yolk !

✎

Stop ! This is a one-way street !

Well, I'm only going one way !

Yes, but everyone else is going the other way !

Well, you're a policeman, make them turn round !

✎

What is the thing that is most read at Christmas ?

Rudolph's nose !

How do penguins get to school?

On 21 speed mountain icicles!

✎

Why do cows have horns?

Because they would look pretty silly with bells on their heads!

✎

Mary had a little lamb,
which she dressed in pretty blouses,
she also had a ferret,
which she put down her dad's trousers!

What goes MOOOOOZ ?

A jet flying backwards !

What do blacksmiths eat for breakfast ?

Vice Crispies !

Why do toolmakers always escape from fires ?

They know the drill !

What self defence method do mice use ?

Ka - rat - e !

What did the stupid burglar do when he saw a 'WANTED' poster outside the police station?

He went in and applied for the job!

✎

What is a big game hunter?

Someone who can't find the football stadium!

30 people were sheltering under an umbrella, how many of them got wet ?

None - it wasn't raining !

✎

Why are burglars such good tennis players ?

Because they spend such a lot of their time in courts !

Is that a new perfume I smell ?

It is, and you do !

What do vampires use to phone relatives ?

A terror - phone !

What are wasps favourite flowers ?

Bee - gonias !

Why did the fly fly ?

Because the spider spied her !

What sort of monster is musical ?

The one with A Flat head !

Where do Chinese vampires live ?

Fang - Hai !

Why did the Romans build straight roads ?

They didn't want anyone hiding round the corners !

✎

What do you call a dinosaur that
keeps you awake at night ?

Bronto - snore - us !

✎

What is the name of the Australian dog drummer ?

Dingo Starr !

AWFUL ALPHABETS

A

Artichoke - a joke that artists tell each other!

Abacus - swear word used by an aba!

Address Book - large book where women keep their clothes!

Aeroplane - tool used to make wooden flying machines!

Agent - someone who is polite!

Alarm clock - timepiece that scares everybody!

Algebra - underwear worn by female alge!

Ambush - place where pigs like to sleep!

Appetite - when you can't eat because your belt is too tight!

Astronaut - nothing in space!

B

Baby - small bee!

Batchelor - unmarried vampire!

Bacon - what you eat on fry day!

Ballet - form of entertainment that is tu tu wonderful!

Bank - side of river where voles keep their money!

Barbecue - line of people waiting to buy toy dolls!

Bark - the sound a tree makes!

Bat - what vampires use to play cricket with!

Battery - what the school cook was arrested for!

Bed - where the idiot planted his light bulbs!

Bell - the kids round here will steal anything - now the school bell's gone!

Bewitched - a bee that has upset a witch!

Bookworm - something that is always having to eat its words!

Boomerang - a bent stick that is impossible to throw away!

Boxer - dog that starts punching when it hears a bell ring!

Bricklayer - chicken fed on sand and cement!

Broomstick - something that makes witches fly off the handle!

Buffalo - similar to a bison, but you can't wash your hands in a buffalo!

Bulldog - like a sheepdog - but for cows!

Butter - another name for goat!

C

Cabbage - how old a taxi is!

Camel - plural = camelot!

Canary - bird that comes in a tin!

Cannibal - someone who is always pleased to eat you!

Captain - cap that comes in a tin!

Cartoon - a song you sing in the car!

Catapult - weapon used by cats!

Caterpillar - column used to hold up a cat's home!

Cheesecake - served at a mouse's birthday party!

Chicken - something that always speaks with fowl language!

Chirrup of figs - what you give to a constipated budgie!

Circus - knight of old who invented the big top!

Cliff - man with seagulls on his head!

Coconut - someone who loves cocoa!

Coffin - what Dracula does a lot of when he has a cold!

Comb - what bees do their hair with!

Comedian - chicken that tells jokes!

Cowgirl - female cow!

Crocodile - telephone operator for alligators!

Cucumber - curved snooker cue!

D

Dance - something hens do chick to chick!

Dentist - the first thing a vampire bites after having a filling!

Desert - pudding made from sand!

Dinner - Batman's theme tune (Dinner, Dinner, Dinner, Dinner, Batman!)

Dinosaur - pimple on a T. Rex!

Dogfish - cod with a personality problem!

Dogma - mother of puppies!

Dollar Bill - American!

Door catch - splinter that rips clothes when you go into house!

Double glazing - two pairs of glasses!

Draculard - overweight vampire!

Drunk - empty glass!

Dynamite - then again she might not!

E

Ear - the opposite of there!

Eel - downtrodden fish!

Egypt - place where daddies are mummies!

Electrician - someone who does tricks with light bulbs!

Escalator - a moving stairway that makes you late for school!

Eskimo - escalator in a cold place!

F

Face pack - box that ugly people keep their make up in!

Fairy ring - goblin's telephone system!

False teeth - teeth that tell lies!

Fang mail - what a vampire gets through the post!

Fatima - overweight mother!

Feet - what your shoes are when they measure 12 inches!

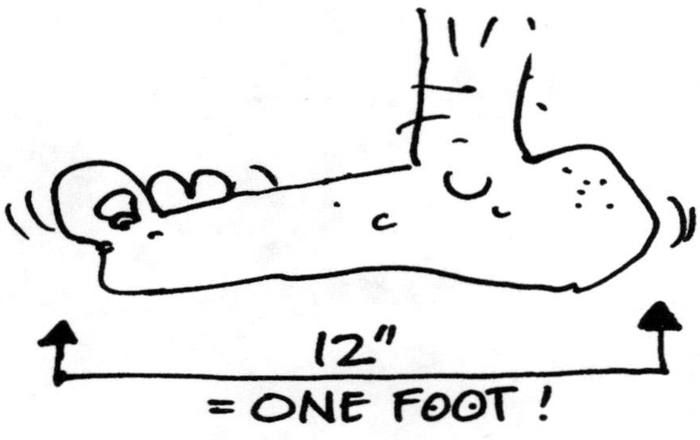

Female - women posties!

Fencing team - people who put up fences!

Fiend - almost a friend!

Filing cabinet - where cannibals keep all the spare fingernails!

Fish and ships - what a sea monster eats!

Flat mate - what you get if you invite a giant monster round for tea!

Floodlight - what Noah had on the ark to see where he was going!

Flu - what an insect does when it has a cold!

Fly paper - what flies read to get the news!

Foghorn - what cows use to find each other in the mist !

Fork Lift Truck - lorry used to pick up a giant's cutlery !

Fortune cookie - expensive biscuit !

Fountain pen - pen that runs on water !

Frankenstein - a self made man!

a man who made his own entertainment!

a man who kept people in stitches!

Frogspawn - a toad's chess piece!

Fur - a type of woolly tree!

Furniture - vege - tables are the sort of furniture that monsters eat!

G

Gamble - what naughty little lambs do!

Gangster - when criminals get together to bake a cake!

Garlic - something to make a vampire cross!

Geography - what you have to pay a geogra to get it to work for you!

Ghost train - what spooks travel on when they go on ghouliday!

Ghould - what spooks score in football!

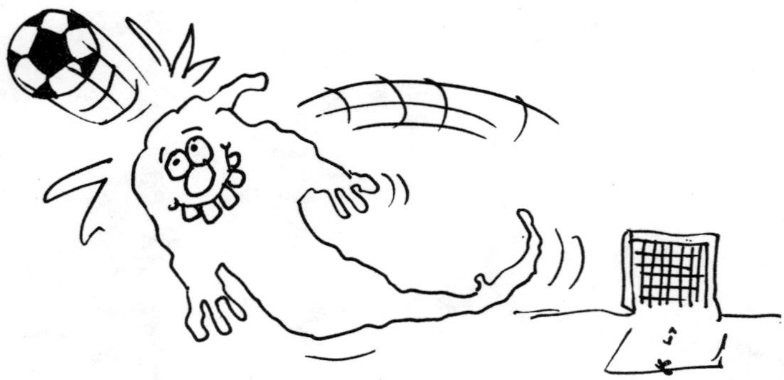

Giant snails - what you find on the end of giant's fingers!

Gruesome - the wrong way to say that your daughter has grown!

Glass eyes - something that might just come out in conversation!

Gnome - a gnouse where elves live!

Goldfish - a fish that ate 24 carrots!

Gorilla - what a chimp puts bread under to make toast!

Granny flat - what you get if you invite a monster round for tea!

Graveyard - grave for a dwarf!

Greece - what the school cook uses!

Greenhouse - home for aliens!

Guillotine - guaranteed cure for dandruff!

H

Hairdresser - cupboard where a bald man keeps his wigs!

Hamlet - pig playing Shakespeare!

Hammock - bed for pigs!

Handicap - neat place to keep your hat!

Haunting - the sort of melodies that ghosts sing to each other!

Headgear - frankenstein's bolts!

Hellfire - get the sack from Satan!

Hindu - a party where you invite all your hin laws!

Hippie - one of the joints in your leggie!

Hole in one - why golfers carry a spare pair of trousers - in case they get a hole in one!

Honeycomb - what bees do their hair with!

Horse - when a pony has a sore throat!

Human beings - what cannibals like to eat on toast!

House - what you shout when you win a cottage at bingo!

I

Ice cream - and so would you if you had just seen a ghost!

Ig - eskimo house without a loo!

Icicle - bicycle with a wheel missing!

Illness - what the Loch Ness monster sometimes catches!

Ink - what you get from a sheep when it's turned into a pen!

Inkling - a baby pen!

Invisible man - someone who has transparents!

Iron tablets - pills that do the laundry!

Italian wine - the sound that ghosts from Milan make!

J

Jack - what you call a man with a car on his head!

Jack Frost - a man with an ice cream van on his head!

Jellyfish - what monsters eat at parties!

Juggler - the vein that Dracula visits the circus to see!

Jumper - a cross between a sheep and a kangaroo!

Jungle sale - where Tarzan buys his clothes!

K

Ketchup - what one sauce bottle shouts to another in a race!

Kick - what some people get out of doing karate!

Konga - a dance for big monkeys!

Kippers - sleeping fish!

Kitten - when a cat tells you a joke!

Knight - what you get if you knit with steel wool!

L

Ladder - the place where very tall people store their food!

Ladybird - female bird!

Lamb chops - what you get from a sheep who knows karate!

Landing - where jumbo jets will end up if you leave the lights on!

Lap - what motor racing cats do a lot of!

Larder - where the school cook keeps all her lard!

Legs - what cannibals love to eat - especially fried legs and bacon!

Lemonade - hearing aid for a lemon!

Lice - what Australians tie up their shoes with!

Lid - what Australians have in their pencils!

Liar - dishonest lute!

Lighthouse - what a snail carries on its back!

Lion - if the lion is engaged you can't make any telephone calls in the jungle!

Lisp - Hith ith the thound a thnake with a lithp makesth!

Lizard - the magician in a snake's circus!

Loaf - what idle bread does!

Lonely heart - missing vampire's parcel!

Lone Ranger - the man who gets you a mortgage!

M

Mad - what happens when a vampire goes batty!

Maggot - a grub's favourite TV detective!

Mailman - opposite of female woman!

Manure - recyclable unmentionables!

Marriage lines - where you tie your wife or husband when a train is coming!

Meatball - what sausages play hockey with!

Meeting of minds - when two monsters run head first into each other!

Memory lapse - when you can't remember how many times you've run round the track!

Mercy - what vampires shout when they are forced to eat garlicky French food!

Mermaid - a fish that mumbles!

Mexican - a can full of mexies!

Mice - how posh people say mouse!

Mole - a furry miner!

Money boxes - underpants that people keep their cash in!

Monkey - what an ape opens his door with!

Moose - pudding made from deer!

Moth ball - dance where butterflies are made welcome!

Mountaineer - what a mountain listens with!

Mummies - daddies with an interest in wrap music!

Mushroom - when your dustbin is full of toadstools, there's not mushroom inside!

N

Nailbiter - monster with a mouth full of metal!

Narrow squeak - the noise you hear when you tread on a thin mouse!

Neck - what vampires in love like to do best!

Necktie - Frankenstein's bolt!

Nervous wreck - a sunken ship with a twitch!

Newspaper - what gnus read!

Night school - where vampires go to learn to read in the dark!

Nit nurse - someone who makes you a nice woolly hat to keep your nits warm!

Noah's ark - the first boat ever fitted with floodlights!

Note paper - for writing down music!

Nun - someone who can hide on a zebra crossing!

O

Octopus - cat with 8 legs!

Oil - there are two types.

Crude Oil - which floats on the sea and shouts "knickers!"

Refined Oil - which floats on the sea and says, quietly, "underpants!"

Oinkment - what you give a pig with pimples!

Onion - from the old saying - "An apple a day keeps the doctor away, an onion a day keeps everyone else away!"

Orangeade - What you give a deaf fruit!

Orchestra - an anagram of CARTHORSE - true!

P

Paddle - how posh people say puddle!

Pane - what you feel when you walk into a sheet of glass!

Parrot - what the Chinese man called the man who flew the plane!

Peach - what you can call anyone with a heart of stone!

Peanuts - the sort of nuts you find in a pod!

Pear - what the French apple called his dad!

Peas - this is what we get at Christmas - peas on earth and goodwill to all men!

Pedestrian - why did the optician build his shop in the new precinct? Because it had been pedestrian - eyes - ed!

Pelican - the sort of tin that pelis are stored in!

Pen - where a farmer keeps his sheep and his ink!

Penguins - something that polar bears never eat - because they can't get the wrappers off!

Phantom - the sort of pen a ghost writes with - a phantom pen!

Phoney - someone who pretends he has a telephone in his pocket!

Piano - something you drop down a mineshaft to get A Flat Minor!

Piece of pie - what's left after the cook has dropped it on the kitchen floor!

Piglet - a small house rented out to pigs!

Pigeon Toes - what you get if you put birdseed in your shoes!

Plumber - drain surgeon!

Poetry in motion - when the teacher throws an English book across the room!

Poison Ivy - the girl who has an effect on just about everybody!

Pole - stick of wood found in the snow!

Policeman - the man who lives at 999, Letsby Avenue!

Porcupine - what you get if you cross a pig and a tropical fruit!

Pork chop - what a pig that knows karate does!

Pottery in motion - when someone throws a plate at you!

Prince - what royalty have to give to the police if they are suspected of a crime - finger prince!

Printer - a job you can only get if you happen to be the right type!

Promise - something that you have to give to other people and keep as well!

Puffin - breathless bird!

Punch clock - how a boxer logs into work each day!

Q

Quack - a duck doctor!

Queen bee - the one with a tiny crown!

Queue jumper - a sweater you give to a cold queue!

Quicksand - builder's material that runs away when you're not looking!

R

Rabbit - when a rabbit gets trapped under a sunbed, is he a hot cross bun ?

Racing pigeon - the one with the crash helmet and the stripes down the wings !

Railway lines - what teachers give naughty railways to do !

Raining cats and dogs - when this happens be careful not to step in a poodle !

Red Indian - a tribe with all the know how they need !

Reincarnation - being born again as a can of evaporated milk !

Religious education exams - these are marked with a spirit level!

Reptile - special flat frogs that stick to bathroom walls!

Restaurant - a cruel place where they beat eggs, batter fish and whip cream!

Revolution - what the wheel caused when it was first invented!

Road hog - pig who drives badly!

Robin Banks - a man who steals for a living!

Robinson Crusoe - a man who took weekends off - because he had all his work done by Friday!

Robot - a thing with nerves of steel!

Rock concert - where you would go to hear The Rolling Stones!

Roller skates - dangerous wheeled fish!

Rome - a city that must have been built at night - because we know it wasn't built in a day!

Rose petal - what you have on a rose bicycle!

Row boat - a boat that sits patiently in line!

Rubbish collection - a job that you just pick up as you go along!

Run over - this will make you feel tyred!

Russia - Knock, knock!
Who's there?
Russia!
Russia who?
Russia way - a monster's coming!

S

Sandwitch - a witch eating her packed lunch on the beach!

Santa claus - The creature who takes presents to monsters!

Saucer - where rivers start
- like the saucer the Nile for example!

Sausage roll - goes with sausage rock to make music!

School dinners - our daily dread!

Scratch card - what you use if you get fleas!

Second hand - what a used wristwatch has!

Secret - something that everyone except you knows!

Shadow boxing - putting shadows into containers!

Sheep dip - what sheep have at parties!

Sherlock Bones - the famous skeleton detective!

Shoe - what you shout to a gang of runaway trainers!

Shorts - half hearted trousers!

Shy - what coconuts are on their first date!

Sick jokes - what people in hospital tell each other!

Sign - seen outside the shipyard - Gone To Launch!

Singing insects - humbugs!

Skateboard - fish used as transport by sharks!

Skeleton staff - people working in a graveyard!

Sledgehammer - what you take to school when you break up!

Sleeping pills - tablets that snore in the bottle!

Sleepers - people who fall asleep on railway tracks!

Slippers - shoes made from banana skins!

Slugs - very squishy, slimy bullets!

Smoker's cough - that's true!

Snails - it's what you find at the end of your fingers!

Soap Opera - what you get if you sing in the bath or shower!

Soldiers - heavily armed sticks of bread that go into action as soon as they see a shell!

Soup - something that turns to gold if you put 14 carrots in it!

Space - what you need between your ears if you want to be an astronaut when you leave school!

Spellbinding - the covers of a witches book!

Spelling - what witches have to learn at school!

Spirit level - what ghosts use to check that their walls are level!

Spook - when a ghost has already spooken!

Squash - the game elephants like to play
- by getting 3 of their friends in a phone box!

Statue - what an idiot calls a telephone!

Stones - the name of a rock band!

Stork - creep up behind a bird with long legs!

String - the sound you hear if your telephone is made from rope!

Styscraper - a multi storey home for pigs!

Sultan - rich oil owning currant!

T

Tables - furniture you can eat - vegetables!

Tailor's Dummy - what a suit maker sucks when he's scared!

Tap dancer - someone who dances in the sink!

Tapeworms - what insects use to measure things!

Tarzan - someone who creeps up on you in the jungle!

Tea cosy - used to keep tea bags feeling comfy!

Teacher's pet - the child kept in the cage by the door!

Teenager - say red backwards - now you are one!

Theatre - where ghosts go to see a phantomime at Christmas!

Thunder - what outdoor orchestras with good conductors should avoid!

Time - a herb with a wristwatch!

Tinder - the Australian for tender !

Toadstools - what toads use for DIY !

Tomorrow - is not a very strong day
- in fact it's a weekday !

Tooth Fairy - the little fairy who will take out all your teeth if you sleep with your head under the pillow !

Toothbrush - what a tooth does its hair with before it goes out !

Tortoise - what our last teacher did !

Trains - things that stop at devil crossings when they travel through monster country !

Trampolining - a sport that's up and down !

Travel Agent - someone that spies go to to book a holiday!

Tree surgeons - 3 people operating on a person at the same time!

Trifle deaf - what you are if you wake up with jelly and cream in your ear!

U

Udder - when you tell a cow a tall story, she'll tell you to pull the udder one!

Umpire - the man who couldn't spell who designed the State Building in America!

Undertakers - people who have a great graveside manner!

Underpants - knickers worn in submarines!

V

Vampire - someone who is a little batty!

Varnish - disappear with a shiny finish!

Vast - the sort of bottom you see on a ship - 'A Vast Behind!'

Vegetable - where vegetarians eat their meals!

Venetian Blind - someone who has forgotten their glasses!

Vet, Vet, Vet - German band!

Vikings - ancient warriors who invented Norse Code!

Vinegar - what a cat will drink to become a sourpuss!

Violins - used in robberies, robberies with violins!

Viper - snake used to clean car windscreen!

Vitamin B - Bee who runs the health food shop!

W

Waiter - the first thing a monster eats in a restaurant!

Waspital - where you take sickly bees!

Watchdog - dog that goes, woof, woof, tick, woof, woof, tick!

Water - someone who cures warts!

Water polo - sport that you need a sea horse for!

Werewolves - that shoud read "we are wolves!"

Whale weigh station - where a whale gets weighed!

Whistle - what bees can't do, which is why they buzz!

Witch doctor - where witches go when they're not well!

Woodworm - something that says "it was nice gnawing you," to your furniture!

X, Y, Z

X- Ray - ray after he gets hit by a bus!

Xylophone - what xylos telephone their mums and dads with!

Yak - talkative animal!

Yankee Doodle - American drawing!

Zombie - undead bee!

Zoo - what animal lawyers do!

SICKLY AND MOROSE

Doctor - Put your tongue out and say Aaaah, please !

Patient - Aaaaah !

Doctor - Yuck ! You're not going to put that thing back in your mouth are you !

WAITER, WAITER.....

Hop into the kitchen and get me some frogs legs !

Fetch me a crocodile sandwich, and make it snappy !

Get me the 24 hour special, and don't be all day about it !

Get me a bacon sandwich - for my porked lunch !

Doctor, doctor, my belly is really fat !

Hmmm. I think you should diet !

Really - what colour would be best ?

How do you keep flies out of your kitchen?

Move the pile of rotting vegetables into the lounge!

✎

Which vegetable can count the highest?

A pot 80!

✎

Who is that at the door?

A man with a wooden leg called Smith!

Really - and what is his other leg called?

✎

Who is that at the door?

A man with one leg!

Tell him to hop it!

Who is that at the door?

A man with no legs!

Sounds like a low down bum to me!

✎

What does the cannibal plastic surgeon charge?

An arm and a leg!

✎

Waiter - why is this dead mouse in my soup?

Terribly sorry, sir, it should be in the pudding!

A man was staying in a spooky hotel, when he was woken in the middle of the night by an eerie voice saying, "when I get you, I'm going to eat you !"

He ran down to the reception desk and demanded an explanation from the manager. The manager went up to the room with him and pulled open the wardrobe door.

Inside was a monster, desperately trying to reach a chocolate bar that he had dropped down the back. He was muttering to himself, "when I get you, I'm going to eat you !"

✎

What do you call exams that have all the answers pencilled in for you ?

Easy S Es !

✎

Why do aliens eat cabbage and sprouts ?

It puts colour in their cheeks !

What do they call the competition when they draw numbered balls out of a lavatory pan?

The National Pottery!

What do bees qualify to make honey?

They have to pass their hiving test!

What are white, scary and enable you to open any door?

Skeleton keys!

What do they call the competition when they draw numbered balls out of an old coffin?

The National Rottery!

What monster lives in a hanky?

The bogeyman!

What sort of people make the best ghosts ?

The ones who are faint hearted !

✎

Did you hear about the monster who carried on the family traditions...

...he was swallowing in his father's footsteps !

✎

What does a vampire say if he is uncertain about something ?

"I'll suck it and see !"

What do you call a baby budgie ?

A Budget !

What do chickens listen to the radio ?

It's their only form of hentertainment !

What sort of teeth can sing in a high voice ?

Falsetto teeth !

Why did the man send his alphabet soup back ?

Because he couldn't find words to describe it !

What sort of music can you listen to in bed ?

Sheet music !

How do fleas train?

They have to start from scratch!

Football manager – why didn't you stop the ball?

Goalkeeper – I thought that's what these nets were here for!

These pavements are really greasy!

That's no surprise – the rain has been dripping all day!

What do you call pigs who write to each other ?

Pen friends !

✎

Excuse me, how long will the next taxi be ?

About 2.3 metres !

✎

What did the dog say when his owner stopped him chewing the newspaper ?

You took the words out of my mouth !

✎

Blenkinsop - what is the definition of dieting ?

Mind over fatter !

✎

I thought you said he was a vet - he knows nothing about animal medicine at all !

I didn't say he was a vet - I said he had a sore throat - he's a hoarse doctor !

What is the only thing that you can lose, and yet still have ?

Your temper !

✎

What has 50 feet but can't walk ?

A tape measure !

✎

What has 100 feet but can't walk, and it's not a tape measure ?

A dead centipede !

✎

What do old fish wear ?

Shawls !

✎

Did you hear about the M.P. who was arrested ?

He tried to take his seat in the House of Commons, but he was seen by the security cameras !

Which profession gets most fringe benefits ?

Hairdressers !

✎

In which job do you get the most perks ?

In a coffee shop !

✎

What runs all day but is never short of breath ?

A train !

✎

Why do surgeons wear masks ?

So that no-one will know who it was if they make a mistake !

When can't you open a locked piano lid ?

When the keys are on the inside !

✎

There is only one thing higher than a king - his crown !

✎

What sort of eggs go into uncharted areas of the world ?

Egg - splorers !

✎

What is a volcano ?

A headless mountain !

✎

What do you call an American dentist ?

A Yank !

✎

Why don't elephants believe in fairy stories ?

They don't hold with mumbo - jumbo !

What is the difference between a blue elephant and an apple ?

Apples aren't blue !

✎

Why do elephants have big ears ?

Because Noddy didn't pay the ransom !

✎

What is huge, grey and has 12 feet ?

3 elephants !

✎

What driver has never passed a test ?

A screwdriver !

✎

What is the biggest mouse ever discovered ?

The hippopotamouse !

Why did the idiot drive his car off the side of a mountain?

Because someone told him that it was fitted with air brakes!

Why was the man laughing, even though his career was in ruins?

He was an archaeologist!

What did the clean dog say to the dirty dog?

Long time no flea!

What do you give a monster with big feet ?

Big shoes !

✎

What sort of holidays do cannibals never go on ?

Self catering !

✎

What do you get if you cross a giant monster with a frog ?

Something that can catch aeroplanes with its tongue !

✎

What do you call a rabbit's pram ?

A buns buggy !

✎

How do worms drive birds crazy ?

By sleeping late - and never being the early bird !

What does a frog do when it dies ?

It croaks !

✎

When frogs see a rainbow they always look for the croak of gold at the end of it !

✎

What sort of shoes do frogs wear in Summer ?

Open toad sandals !

✎

Why was the mother flea depressed ?

All her children had gone to the dogs !

✎

Why should you never go to the laundrette late at night ?

Because you have to remove your clothes 10 minutes before closing time !

Two children were paddling in the sea...

My, your feet are really dirty !

Well, we didn't come on holiday last year so what do you expect !

✎

Why did the cannibals have indigestion ?

He must have eaten someone who disagreed with him !

✎

What did one sardine say to the other sardine when he saw a submarine full of people ?

"You'll never get me into one of those things !"

✎

Did you hear about the guard dog that loved raw onions and garlic ?

His bark was much, much worse than his bite !

What does a vegetarian cannibal eat ?

Swedes !

✎

Did you hear about the cowboy who only wore one spur ?

He wanted his horse to run round in circles !

✎

A woman went into a petshop and asked if she could have a hamster for her son.

"Sorry," replied the shop keeper, "we don't do part exchange !"

✎

Why do ghosts go to the spring sales in the shops ?

They enjoy bargain haunting !

My friend is so stupid that he thinks twice before saying nothing !

✎

This garden is very light !

Yes, that's because I planted a lot of bulbs last year !

✎

Let me tell you the joke about the mind reader....

....what do you mean you've already heard it !

✎

What pets do monsters keep in glass bowls ?

Ghoulfish !

✎

I went to the ghostly circus last night
- to see the fright rope walker !

✎

At what time should you avoid ghostly dogs and cats ?

On the stroke of midnight !

Why are fish monsters musical ?

They have their own set of scales !

✎

Did you hear about the man who ran away with a deer to get married ?

They anteloped !

✎

How do chickens tell their children off ?

They say 'cock-a-doodle-don't do that !'

✎

Is it true that rabbits get their glasses at the hoptician ?

✎

Why did God give Moses some tablets ?

Moses said he had a headache !

What do dogs and trees have in common ?

Bark !

✎

What do plumbers like to do in the garden ?

Plant leeks !

✎

How does a witch tell the time ?

With a witch-watch !

✎

A man was eating fish and chips when a little dog came along and started biting his trouser leg. He looked at the owner of the dog, who was doing nothing about this, and asked if it was all right to throw it a bit.

"Of course you can throw it a bit !" replied the owner.

The man picked up the dog and threw it over a fence into a pond !

How do you hire a car ?

Take the wheels off and stand it on some bricks !

Why did Arnie take a grenade launcher to a birthday party ?

Because someone told him he would have to blow up the balloons !

The bionic android told his doctor that he thought he was going mad!

The doctor examined him, and agreed. "You've got a screw loose all right!"

✎

A man rescued a vampire from drowning, and the vampire bit him as soon as they got onto dry land. What did the man say?

"If that's all the fangs I get. I'll let you drown next time!"

✎

How did the featherweight boxer do in his last fight?

He tickled his opponent till he gave in!

✎

Can you carry on playing football during a flood?

Yes, you just have to bring on your subs!

What does a skeleton eat at a fast food restaurant ?

Ribs !

✎

What is a prickly pear ?

Two hedgehogs !

✎

What do you call a man with a map and a pair of binoculars on his head ?

Seymour Miles !

✎

What do you call an elephant wearing rubber boots ?

A wellyphant !

✎

Caroline just got the sack. She worked for 8 hours a day, and she slept for 8 hours a day.

Unfortunately they were the same 8 hours !

I like the simple things in life!

Wow, you'll love my sister!

What time did your wristwatch stop?

I don't know, I wasn't looking!

What do bees do when they move into a new hive?

They have a house swarming party!

My wife thinks she's a door
- I think she's just a bit unhinged!

"Would you say your sister was pretty or ugly ?"

"Both !"

"How can she be both ?"

"She's pretty ugly !"

✎

What do you call a woman with a chimney on her head ?

Ruth !

✎

A gorilla went into a quiet country restaurant, and ordered a cup of tea.

He gave the waitress a £10 note and she, thinking that the gorilla was probably a bit stupid, gave the gorilla just £3 change.

"We don't get a lot of gorillas in here," she said.

"I'm not surprised," replied the gorilla, "when you charge £7 for a cup of tea !"

2 men talking in hospital...

"I see they've brought in another case of diarrhoea !"

"Well, let's hope it tastes better than the tea they usually give us at bedtime !"

Whenever I'm down in the dumps,
I buy myself some new clothes !

Ah ! So that's where you get them from !

My teacher, Miss Smith, took up bodybuilding recently.

In fact, she did so well at it that she's now Mr Smith !

Where is the easiest place to find diamonds ?

In a pack of cards !

The opera singer's voice filled the hall
- and then emptied it !

✎

A policeman stopped a car on the motorway.

"Do you realise that you were driving at 90 miles an hour ?"

"I can't have been, I only left my house 10 minutes ago !"

✎

Which knight designed tombs ?

Sir Cophagus !

✎

Which famous artist invented fizzy drinks ?

Lemonado Da Vinci !

✎

"Mum, please may we make mud pies ?"

"Yes, dear, but remember to wash your hands before you eat them !"

Doctor, doctor, I've got a button stuck up my nose, what should I do ?

Breathe through the 4 little holes !

✎

First cat -Where do fleas go in the winter ?

Second cat -Search me !

✎

Why do vampires like funerals ?

Because every shroud has a silver lining !

✎

Which two letters are bad for your teeth ?

D K !

✎

How do you keep an idiot entertained for hours on end ?

Just give him a piece of paper with 'PLEASE TURN OVER' on both sides !

"You're late for school again!"

"I sprained my ankle!"

"What a lame excuse!"

✎

What sport did Frankenstein's monster compete in?

The Pole Volt!

✎

What happened to the naughty witch at school?

She was ex - spelled!

What do you give a sick snake ?

Asp - rin !

✎

"Blenkinsop - you asked for the afternoon off yesterday to go and see your doctor.

Yet I saw you going into a football match with a friend !"

"The doctor is my friend !"

✎

"I got a puncture driving here today !"

"I told you to watch out for that fork in the road !"

✎

What did the curtain say to the window ?

"I've got you covered !"

✎

What did the big chimney say to the little chimney ?

"You're far too young to smoke !"

I could never be in the submarine service – I have to sleep with the windows open!

✎

Dumb Dan was given the job of painting the college flag-pole, but he didn't know how to work out how much paint he would need.

"Lay it on the floor and measure it," suggested a friend.

"Don't be stupid," replied Dan, "I need to know the height not the length!"

✎

Why did the idiot take his windows to the shop?

He wanted them measuring for new curtains!

Did you hear about the idiot who simply could not do decimals - for some reason he could never see the point !

Why do cows lie down when it rains ?

To keep each udder dry !

My dog is a real problem. He chases everything and anything on a bike ! I don't know what to do !

Just take his bike away !

Why are vampires good comedians ?

They have a biting wit !

✎

My dog saw a sign that said "wet paint",
and so he did just that !

✎

Why are toilet seats so cheap at the moment ?

I don't know, I suppose the bottom must have dropped out of the market !

✎

My son has just been accepted by a medical school -

but they don't want him while he's alive !

✎

Why was the surgeon working on the road ?

It needed a by-pass !

What do you call an alien with two heads?

A two-headed alien!

What do aliens do with humans they find in space ships?

Put them in the larder - they keep tinned food for emergencies!

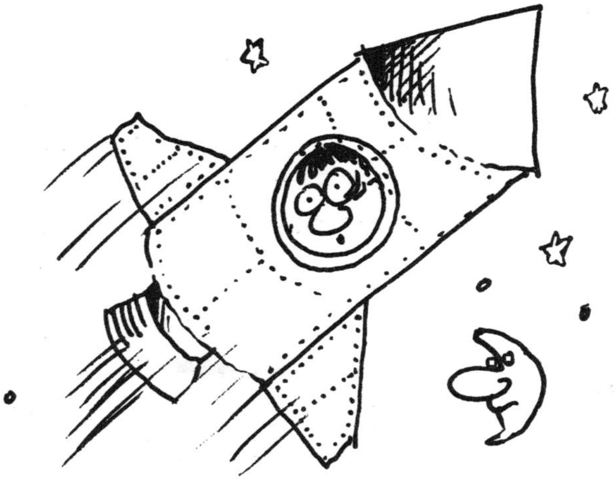

What should you do if you find a green alien?

Wait until it's ripe!

Why do aliens have seven fingers on each hand?

Because otherwise they would have two empty fingers in each glove!

Where do aliens live?

In green houses!

What lights do aliens switch on every Saturday?

Satellites!

What game do aliens play to while away the hours in deep space?

Moonopoly!

Where do alien children go in the evenings ?

Rocket and Roll concerts !

What are wealthy aliens members of ?

The Jet Set !

Where do aliens go to study their GCSEs ?

High School (Very High School) !

Why do aliens never starve in space ?

Because they always know where to find a Mars, a Galaxy and a Milky Way !

What do evil aliens eat for lunch ?

Beans on toast - (Human Beans on toast) !

Why are aliens good for the environment ?

Because they are green !

What do aliens have to do before they can drive a rocket at twice the speed of light in deep space ?

Reverse it out of the garage !

What do aliens call junk food?

Unidentified Frying Objects!

✎

How do you know when aliens are envious?

Easy - they turn green!

✎

What sort of sweets do Martians eat?

Martian mallows!

✎

Where do aliens go to study rocket science?

Mooniversity!

✎

How do you know when an alien is homesick?

He just moons about all over the place!

What do you give a sick alien ?

Planetcetamol !

✎

Which railway company employs ghosts ?

British Wail !

✎

How do you contact someone who lives on Saturn ?

Give them a ring !

✎

What is the quickest way to get an alien baby to sleep ?

Rocket !

Alien School Report

Music	He loves the Planet Suite by Holst !
Chemistry	Blew off one of his heads making rocket fuel !
Martian	KLargin SCRung,jlkfr TTTTugt KLMgg FRelOOmmMw~We TTrRaaakk !
Maths	Can count up to seventeen using the fingers on his left hand !
Space	Takes a bite out of the Milky Way every time he goes there on a school trip !

What do you call an alien girl band?

The Space Girls!

What do you call a mad alien?

A Lunar-tic!

What is the name of the planet inhabited by video recorders?

Planet of the Tapes!

What ticket do you ask for to go there for a holiday?

Return to the Planet of the Tapes!

What game do nasty aliens play with Earth spaceships ?

Shuttlecocks !

✎

Which side of a spaceship passes closest to the planets ?

The Outside !

✎

Why did the impressionist crash through the ceiling ?

He was taking off a rocket taking off !

What does an alien gardener do with his hedges ?

Eclipse them every Spring !

Why did the alien buy a pocket computer ?

So he could work out how many pockets he has !

✎

How can you tell if a computer is disgruntled ?

It will have a chip on its shoulder !

✎

How do you get directions in deep space ?

Askeroid !

Where do aliens keep fish they capture from other planets?

In a planetarium!

Why did the alien school have no computers?

Because someone ate all the apples!

What do evil aliens grind up to make a hot drink?

Coffee beings!

What do you call an alien who travels through space on a ketchup bottle ?

A flying saucer !

✎

Why did the attendant turn space ships away from the lunar car park ?

It was a full moon !

✎

How does a Martian know he's attractive ?

When bits of metal stick to him !

What do you call a space ship made from cow pats?

A Pooh F O!

Where do alien space ship pilots go to learn how to fly in the darkness of outer space?

Night school!

What do you call a sad space ship?

An unidentified crying object!

What does the alien from planet X use to smooth her nails?

The X Files, of course!

Why did the bakers work late ?

Because they kneaded the dough !

✎

Why are alien gardeners so good ?

Because they have green fingers !

✎

What do alien children do on Halloween ?

They go from door to door dressed as humans !

How do you know if there is an alien in your house?

There will be a spaceship parked in the garden!

How do you communicate with aliens out in deep space?

You have to shout really loudly!

How do you tell if an alien is embarrassed?

They blush - and their cheeks go purple!

How do you catch a Venusian mega mouse ?

In a Venusian mega mouse-trap !

✎

What do you give a sick alien ?

Paracetamoons !

✎

Where do aliens do their shopping ?

In a greengrocers !

✎

Why do some aliens make their space ships out of twisted planks of wood ?

So they can travel at warp speed !

✎

Who is in love with the alien James Bond ?

Miss Mooneypenny !

Where do aliens go for holidays?

Lanzarocket!

What do aliens put on their cakes?

Mars - ipan!

Who is the alien's favourite robot cartoon character?

Tin - Tin!

Why was the robot rubbing its joints with a video?

Because it was a video of Grease!

What is a robot's favourite chocolate?

Whole Nut!

Where are parts for robots made?

In Bolton, Knutsford and Leeds!

What do you give a robot who fancies a light snack?

Some 60 watt bulbs!

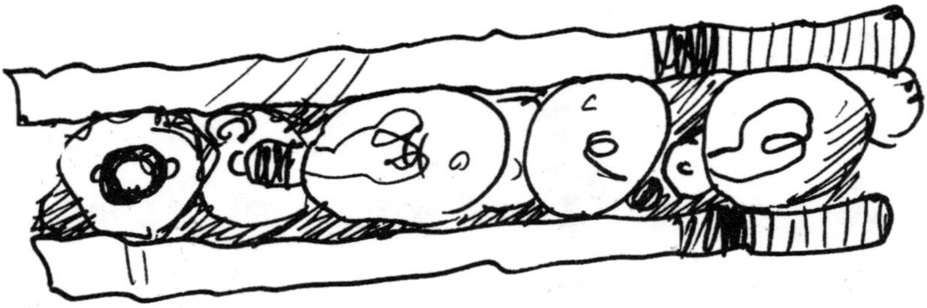

What did the teacher give the alien monster for lunch?

Class 4B!

What sort of music do robots like best?

Steel band music!

Who do robots vote for in a General Election?

Tinny Blair!

How do you know when a robot
has been in your fridge ?

There are footprints in the butter !

How do you invite a robot to a party ?

Send round a tinvitation !

What firework do aliens like best ?

Rockets !

What do you call a deer with its eyes poked out ?

No eye deer !

What is an alien's favourite TV programme ?

Blind date - it's the only way they can get a human girlfriend !

What do you call computer controlled sandpaper ?

Science Friction !

If you get lost in space - who should
you ask for directions ?

**An alien hairdresser -
they know all the short cuts !**

✎

If an alien leaves his chewing gum orbiting
the Earth - what
do you call it ?

A Chew - F - O !

✎

Your son will make an
excellent rocket pilot !

Why do you say that ?

He has nothing but
space between his ears !

✎

Why do steel robots have so many friends ?

I suppose they must have magnetic personalities !

What do daleks drink?

Exterminade!

What do aliens put on their toast?

Mars - malade!

Where is the smelliest part of an alien spaceship?

The Com - poooh - ter!

Why did the alien paint his spaceship with sugar and vinegar ?

He wanted a sweet and sour saucer !

✎

How do you tip an alien spaceship over ?

Rocket !

✎

What did the greedy alien say when he landed on a new planet ?

Take me to your larder !

What dance can you see in the night sky ?

The Moon Walk !

✎

Why did the football manager want to get in touch with the alien ?

Because he knew where all the shooting stars were !

✎

What did the mummy robot say to her children ?

Look before you bleep !

✎

Why was the young robot so happy ?

Because he didn't have a chip on his shoulder !

Where does the alien gardener keep his tools ?

In an astro - hut !

Where do Martians go to see a movie ?

Cine - mars !

Knock, knock,
Who's there ?
Jupiter
Jupiter Who ?
Jupiter spaceship on my lawn ?

What is worse than finding a 12 legged Venusian mega - maggot in your apple ?

Finding half a 12 legged Venusian mega - maggot in your apple !

What did the referee book the alien for ?

Hand ball, Hand ball, Hand ball, Hand ball....

What do aliens use to go up and down ?

Stairs !

Where did they put the alien who stole a field full of rhubarb?

In Custardy!

✎

What is green and very noisy?

An alien with a drum kit!

✎

Who was the first man on the moon?

A Spaceman!

What did one rocket say to the other ?

I wish I could stop smoking !

I don't know what to buy my pal, the space alien, for his birthday ?

How about 5 pairs of slippers !

Why do astronauts never eat after take off ?

Because they have just had a big launch !

MAD MISCELLANY

What is furry and smells of mint ?

A Polo bear !

✎

What do sparrows eat for breakfast ?

Tweet a Bix !

✎

What do cats eat for breakfast ?

Shredded Tweet !

✎

What does Doctor Jeckyll do on hoilday ?

He tans his Hyde !

✎

"Doctor, I can't get to sleep at night !"

"Sleep on a window sill - you'll soon drop off !"

Which Russian leader was round and purple ?

Alexander the grape !

What will you get if you swallow plutonium ?

Atomic ache !

What is a bunsen burner for ?

Setting fire to bunsens ?

Why did the boy go to boarding school?

Because he was always bored!

✎

"Have you put some more water in the goldfish bowl?"

"No, it hasn't drunk the water I put in 6 months ago yet!"

✎

"Blenkinsop, you've been coming to my piano lessons for 6 months now, and I think it's time I told you - you aren't supposed to blow it!"

✎

He is the sort of man that girls look at twice - they can't believe he is so ugly the first time!

✎

How does an idiot get to the top of a tree?

Stands on an acorn and waits for it to grow!

What do frogs drink at bedtime?

Croako!

✎

Do old bicycles get recycled?

✎

Do old car tyres get retired?

✎

Roses are red
Violets are blue
You look like a codfish
And smell like one too!

✎

Why was the fish so happy?

Because he was moving to a new plaice!

What do baby fish eat on their birthday ?

Fish Cakes !

✎

Knock, knock...
Who's there ?
Cod...
Cod who ?
Cod a minute to spare ?

✎

Knock, knock...
Who's there ?
Plaice...
Plaice who ?
Plaice to see you !

✎

Knock, knock...
Who's there ?
Haddock...
Haddock who ?
Haddock 'nuff of this – I'm off !

Knock, knock...
Who's there ?
Eel...
Eel who ?
Eel be here in a minute - open the door !

Knock, knock...
Who's there ?
Salmon...
Salmon who ?
Salmon Dave !

Knock, knock...
Who's there ?
Crab...
Crab who ?
Crab the door handle and pull !

Knock, knock...
Who's there?
I'm just sturgeon...
I'm just sturgeon who?
I'm just sturgeon you to open the door!

✎

Knock, knock...
Who's there?
Whale...
Whale who?
Whale meet again!

✎

Knock, knock...
Who's there?
Dolphin...
Dolphin who?
Dolphin you can get away with this!

✎

Knock, knock...
Who's there?
You shut the door...
You shut the door who?
You shut the door on Porpoise!

Knock, knock...
Who's there?
Lobster...
Lobster who?
Lobster key out through the window and I'll open it!

Knock, knock...
Who's there?
Al Kipper...
Al Kipper who?
Al Kipper few days here if that's OK!

Knock, knock...
Who's there?
Minnow...
Minnow who?
Minnow you're in there!

Knock, knock...
Who's there ?
The Seaweed...
The Seaweed who ?
The Seaweed, so I need to come in and get dry !

✎

Knock, knock...
Who's there ?
Trout...
Trout who ?
Trout the day I've been waiting here !

✎

Knock, knock...
Who's there ?
Wave...
Wave who ?
Wave got tired of waiting - we're off !

✎

Knock, knock...
Who's there ?
Piranha...
Piranha who ?
Piranha kettle and we'll have a nice cup of tea !

Knock, knock...
Who's there?
Cod roe...
Cod roe who?
Cod roe nation street is on the telly!

Knock, knock...
Who's there?
Whale...
Whale who?
Whale have a different sort of joke now...

What do gnomes eat at birthday parties?

Fairy cakes!

Who is the strongest man in the world?

A policeman - he can hold up a whole streetful of traffic with one hand!

✎

What part of your body is curry good for?

Your Tikka!

✎

What should you never do when you see a dentist?

Take your cap off!

✎

What is the name of the detective that Shakespeare invented?

Shylock Holmes!

✎

A space monster's mum was complaining about the number of sweets he ate...

"You've had two Mars, a Milky Way and you're halfway through a Galaxy!"

What do you call a bear without a beard ?

A bare faced bear !

✎

What happened when the piano fell on the army barracks ?

There was A flat Major !

✎

What time is it when you're hungry ?

Something to eat !

✎

What came between the Iron Age and the Stone Age ?

The cabbage ?

✎

What do you call a mad squirrel ?

Nuts !

What did the rabbit say when it went bald ?

Hare today, gone tomorrow !

What does a girl say when she's going out with a bear ?

We're going teddy !

How can you send a liquid through the post in an ordinary letter ?

When it's T !

What is big and grey and wobbly ?

A jellyphant !

Why was the pop group thrown out of the nightclub by the bouncer ?

They were an elastic band !

What wears a sock on its bottom ?

Your leg !

Why was the idiot feeding his chickens haggis ?

He wanted them to lay Scotch eggs !

What is the only thing you can have in an empty pocket ?

A Hole !

What sort of music do very, very cold people listen to?

The Blues!

✎

"A robber, who stole three thousand bars of soap, has made a clean getaway!"

✎

Waiter - there's a dead mouse in my salad!

It's the rubbish food in this place that kills them, sir!

✎

Why did the elephant refuse to play cards with his two friends?

Because one of them was lion and the other was a cheetah!

Waiter - what are these two worms on my plate ?

They are the sausages, sir !

How do you stop moles from digging up your lawn ?

Lock the toolshed !

What's black and white, and wet at the bottom ?

A nun paddling in the sea !

Why are ducks so miserable ?

They always have down in the mouth !

✎

What goes oom, oom, oom ?

A cow walking backwards !

✎

Why do bees buzz ?

Because they can never remember the words !

✎

What sort of crossword clues does Dracula like ?

Cryptic ones !

✎

How does the queen of the sea travel around her kingdom ?

By Octobus !

Mary had a little lamb,
She ate it with mint sauce!
If she buys a jar of mustard,
I'd watch out, mister horse!

How do you make a sausage roll?

Push it down a steep hill!

Where do space aliens keep their video collections?

Planet of the tapes!

Waiter - there's half a dead cockroach in my food!

You'll have to pay for the half you've eaten, Sir!

✎

What sort of toys are rude?

Teddies - because they go around bear!

✎

Why was the ugly monster called Isaiah?

Because one eye's higher than the other!

Why is the leopard the only animal that can't hide from hunters?

Because it's always spotted!

✎

What do aliens go to watch at the movies?

Starzan!

✎

How do you know when a dog is housetrained?

It leaves its little poodles outside!

✎

What do monsters eat for breakfast?

Lice Crispies!

✎

4 kippers please, and leave the eyes in
- I'll need something to see me through the week!

Where are school dinners served?

The Mushroom!

✎

With alphabet soup,
you can spell your name,
you can write rude words,
again and again.
With alphabet soup,
take it or leave it,
whatever you spell,
you know you'll have to eat it!

✎

How do you survive an electric shock?

Call the operator and ask them to reverse the charge!

✎

What sort of bird can see round corners?

A Crane!

A young man was sitting by the fire watching the kettle boil...

"If only we could harness this wonderful power of steam, perhaps one day we could even use it to drive vehicles and carry people from one town to another..."

His mother called out to him...

"Hurry up and get dressed or you'll miss the train to work again!"

✎

Where is the best place to keep a pie?

Your tummy!

What building drips cheese and tomatoes
onto the town beneath ?

The leaning tower of Pizza !

Why couldn't Noah, his son and his wife all go fishing ?

He only had two worms !

Did you hear about the orchestra leader who
survived being hit by lightning ?

Fortunately he was a very bad conductor !

What is green and hot and goes
round and round ?

An alien in a tumble drier !

Why are babies so good at football ?

**Because they know how to dribble from the moment
they are born !**

Did you hear about the stupid robber ?

He threw a brick through the jewellers window on Monday night, and then came back and did the same again on Tuesday night – someone told him that the window had double glazing !

✎

What are round and pink and wear trainers ?

Jogging bottoms !

✎

Doctor, doctor, my wife thinks she's a *jumbo jet* !

Don't be silly – she isn't even an elephant !

What do bad comedians eat at breakfast ?

Corny flakes !

✎

Why did the alien turn the restaurant waiter upside down ?

Someone told him that you had to tip the waiter !

✎

Why did the witch put her broomstick in the fridge ?

She fancied a cold spell !

✎

Which holiday camp do goats go to ?

Buttlins !

✎

Where do electricians go on holiday ?

Leeds !

Where do meccano enthusiasts go on holiday ?

Bolton !

✎

Where do policemen go on holiday ?

The Copper Cobana Beach !

✎

How do fish go on holiday ?

By Whale way !

✎

How do cavemen get to know each other ?

By joining clubs !

✎

What do you call frozen mice ?

Micicles !

What is a shark's favourite pudding ?

Spotted Dick - so if you are called Dick, make sure they don't spot you !

✎

Doctor, doctor, my little boy has swallowed my wristwatch !

Don't worry, we will soon see the passage of time !

✎

What do idiot's have for pudding ?

Clotted Dick !

✎

What did the woman say to the masked man working in her local bank ?

I'd like to see the loan arranger, Lone Ranger !

✎

Why do posties like Z ?

Because there aren't any more letters after it !

What did the maths teacher do when his nose got blocked?

He worked it out with his pencil and ruler!

How do you keep an idiot in suspense?

I'll tell you on page 2,890!

What does an elephant do when it has diarrhoea?

Goes to the toilet!

What do you call a wizard on a broomstick ?

A Flying Sorcerer !

✎

What exams are gardeners good at ?

Hoe levels !

✎

What exams are Santa's good at ?

Ho, Ho, Ho levels !

✎

Why were the carpenter's teeth chipped ?

Because he was always biting his nails !

What is a jelly baby's favourite sweet ?

Chewing gum !

✎

What did the vampire doctor say ?

Necks please !

✎

Two oranges were playing tennis - it was 40 all - what did the umpire shout ?

Juice !

✎

Why does Dracula never intend to get married ?

He is a bat - chelor !

✎

What happened to the football that was kicked close to a fan ?

It blew out of the stadium !

What sort of car does an alligator drive ?

Some old crock !

✎

What job did the spider get ?

A web designer !

✎

What do you get if you cross a warlock and a PC ?

A computer wizard !

✎

What do you get if you cross a dinosaur with a fish ?

Jurassic shark !

✎

What does an Italian pirate's parrot say ?

Pizzas of eight, pizzas of eight !

When Mary had a little lamb,
the doctor was surprised,
but when Old Macdonald had a farm,
he just couldn't believe his eyes!

Little Jack Horner,
sat in the corner,
eating his Christmas pie.
Along came a spider,
and sat down beside him,
and said "I think I'm in the wrong poem here!"

What do cannibals do at a wedding?

Toast the bridesmaids!

What sort of jungle animal works on the railways ?

A railway lion !

✎

What is the best time of year to pick apples and pears ?

Summer - that's when the farmer is away on holiday !

✎

What pen does a hairless man use ?

A bald point !

✎

Where are you allowed to eat toffees ?

On a chew - chew train !

✎

Where do cats sleep ?

On a caterpillar !

Why should you always laugh when a vampire tells you a joke?

Because they like people to get the point!

What sort of posters do naughty teddies find themselves on?

Wan = Ted posters!

What do you get out of a poorly piano?

A sick note!

What does Tarzan eat ?

Fish and chimps !

Where does Tarzan buy his clothes ?

At a jungle sale !

Where does Tarzan the vampire bite people ?

In the Jungular !

What were Tarzan's last words ?

"Who put grease on that vine...?"

Where does Tarzan buy his loincloths ?

From an end of loin sale !

What did the man say when he walked into the bar ?

OOF ! (It was metal bar !)

✎

Why can't pigs ever get a good radio or TV signal ?

There's always too much cracklin !

✎

What do you find in an angry sewing machine ?

Cross stitches !

✎

Why did the idiot come top of the class at school ?

He was the only one who passed the dope test !

What fish went to music college ?

The piano tuna !

✎

Can you swim on a full stomach ?

Yes, but it's easier to do it in water !

✎

What do you call a monster made of crisps ?

Russell !

✎

What exams do wizards do at school ?

Spelling !

✎

What do you call a vampire's hanky ?

A Neckerchief !

What do you call a vampire who wears a raincoat ?

Count Macula !

✎

What do you call a vampire who lives in a suitcase ?

Count Packula !

✎

What do you call a vampire who likes doing housework ?

Count Vac - ula !

✎

What do you call a vampire who eats nails ?

Count Tackula !

✎

What do you call a vampire who wakes you up to go to school ?

Count Draculalarm !

What do you call a vampire who eats cakes all day ?

Count Dracutart !

✎

Why did the idiot throw a bucket of water into the wardrobe ?

Someone told him there was a smoking jacket in there !

✎

What sort of vampires are interested in sport ?

Football fangs !

✎

How did the skeleton escape being eaten by a dog ?

It was a marrow escape !

✎

Why is the school orchestra in China ?

Because they made the mistake of asking if the audience had any requests !

What is white, scary and soft ?

A jellyton !

✎

What is white, scary and swims round in the sea ?

A skellyfish !

✎

Why is the man with the photographic memory so miserable ?

He has negative thoughts !

What weighs two and a half tons, is grey, and floats gracefully through the air ?

A Hang Gliding Elephant !

What's the worst thing about being a millipede ?

Washing your hands before tea !

A man went into a pet shop and asked the assistant if he could have a hamster for his son.

"Sorry, sir" replied the assistant, "we don't do part-exchanges."

What did the earwig sing as it went to a football match?

Earwig - go, earwig - go, earwig - go....

What is worse than finding a slug in your salad sandwich?

Finding half a slug!

What do you call an 85 year old ant?

An antique!

What happens when there is a stampede
of cows on the motorway ?

There is udder chaos !

Where do you keep a pet vampire fish ?

In your blood stream !

Have you ever hunted bear ?

No, it's far too cold in this part of the world for that !

A cat just scratched my leg!

Shall I put some cream on it?

No, it will be miles away by now!

What is big and grey and has yellow feet?

An elephant standing in custard!

What is grey, has a trunk and travels at 125 miles an hour?

A businessman on a fast train!

How did your budgie die?

Flu!

Don't be daft, budgies can't die from flu!

This one did – it flu under a steam roller!

What fish can you see in the sky?

A Starfish!

Where do kippers go to be cured?

They go to the local sturgeon!

Waiter – this crab only has one claw!

Sorry, sir, it must have been in a fight!

In that case, take this away and bring me the winner!

Doctor, doctor, I think I'm a cat!

How long have you felt like this?

Since I was a kitten!

What time is it when an elephant sits on your fence?

Time to get a new fence!

Doctor, doctor, I think I'm a crocodile!

Don't worry, you'll soon snap out of it!

What does it mean if your nose starts to run?

It's trying to catch a cold!

What do you call a worm in a fur coat?

A caterpillar!

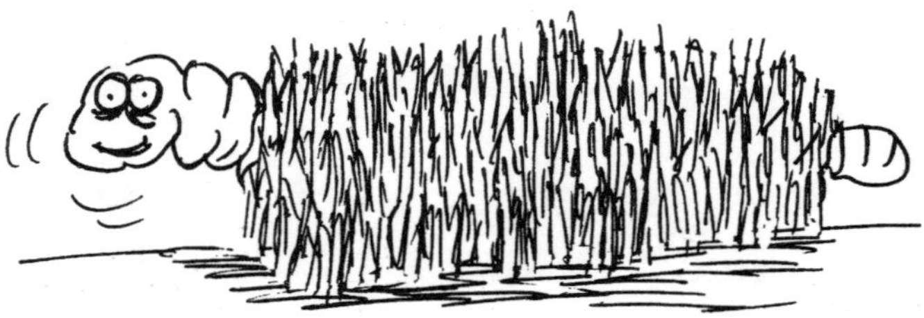

Help, I've lost my cat!

Well, why don't you put an advert in the local newspaper?

Don't be silly - cats can't read!

Eric, what is a prickly pear ?

Er....two porcupines ?

✎

Why do crabs walk sideways ?

Because they had to take some medicine which had side effects !

✎

What sort of insects don't know the words to songs ?

Hum bugs !

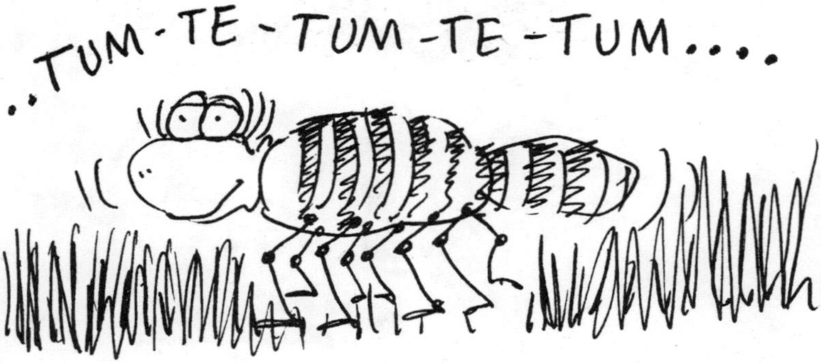

A frog went to the doctor with a sore throat, the doctor examined him and said..."you've got a person in your throat!"

Where do ducks keep their savings?

In river banks!

My dog often goes for a tramp in the woods - and the tramp is getting a bit fed up with it!

What is the easiest way to get an elephant to follow you home?

Just act like a nut!

✎

What do you call a dog that thinks it's a sheep?

Baaaaaking mad!

✎

What went into the lion's cage at the zoo and came out without a scratch?

Another lion!

✎

First cow - Are you worried about this mad cow disease?

Second cow - Doesn't worry me, I'm Napoleon Bonaparte!

✎

How do chimps make toast?

Put it under a gorilla!

What goes bark, tick, bark, tick, bark, tick....

A watchdog !

✎

What is grey and highly dangerous ?

An elephant with a hand grenade !

✎

What did the dog say when its basket was lined with sandpaper ?

Ruff, ruff !

How can you tell the difference between an African elephant and an Indian elephant ?

Look at their passports !

✎

What do you get when you cross a snake with a magician ?

Abra - the - Cobra !

✎

How many pigs do you need to make a smell ?

A Phew !

What is striped and keeps hearing a ringing sound ?

A zebra trapped in a telephone box !

What do ferrets have that no other creatures have ?

Baby ferrets !

What did the pig wear to the fancy dinner dance ?

A pig's - tie !

A man ran over a cat. He apologised to the owner and said that he would be happy to replace it !

'How good are you at catching mice ?' the owner asked him !

How do you keep flies out of the kitchen?

Put a load of manure in the dining room!

✎

How can you cook chicken that really tickles the palate?

Leave the feathers on!

✎

How does a horse tell a joke?

In a jockey - lar fashion!

What do pigs call bath night ?

Hog wash !

✎

How many sheep does it take to make a woolly cardigan ?

I didn't know sheep could knit !

✎

How do snails get ready for a special night out ?

They put on snail varnish !

What do you get if a whale sleeps in your bed?

A wet duvet!

What is a grasshopper?

A cricket on a pogo stick!

Which insect can stay underwater for hours at a time?

A spider in a submarine!

Robert, you can't keep a pig in your bedroom – what about the terrible smell?

Don't worry, he'll soon get used to it!

Why do kangaroos hate bad weather ?

Because the kids have to play inside !

Why was your dog growling at me all through the meal ?

Don't worry, he always does that when people use his favourite plate !

What do you shout to rabbits getting on a ship ?

Bun - voyage !

When is a stray cat likely to come into your home ?

When you leave the door open !

✎

Why did the girl have a pile of dirt on her shoulder ?

Because she had a mole on her cheek !

✎

Waiter, waiter, what is this spider doing in my salad ?

Looking for the flies we usually have in there !

✎

What happens when a frog breaks down ?

It gets toad away !

✎

How do you stop a skunk from smelling ?

Put a peg over its nose !

✎

What sort of animal are you never allowed to take into school exams ?

A Cheetah !

What's black and white and red?

A zebra with nappy rash!

✎

There's a stick insect in my salad – fetch me the branch manager at once!

✎

How do you eat your turkey dinner?

I just gobble it down!

✎

Waiter, waiter, there's a button in my lettuce!

Ah! That will be from the salad dressing sir!

What do monkeys do at the theatre ?

They ape - plaud !

✎

Mmm ! This bread is lovely and warm !

It should be, the cat has been sitting on it all afternoon !

✎

How do you find a lost dog ?

Make a noise like a bone !

They make a perfect couple - He has a chip on his shouder, and there's something fishy about her !

✎

What sound does a Chinese frog make ?

Cloak !

✎

Where does a six foot parrot sleep ?

Wherever it wants to !

✎

Is that a bulldog ?

No, it's a Labrador, but it ran into a wall chasing a cat !

✎

What sort of dog has no tail ?

A hot dog !

A man slipped when working on his roof, and was hanging onto the window ledge by his fingertips. He saw the cat through the window and called out to it to get help.

The cat said 'me ? how ?'

✎

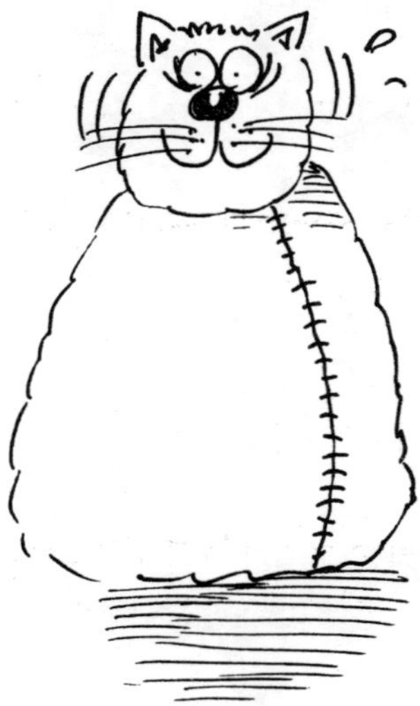

Why is a cat bigger at night than during the day ?

Because its owner lets it out at night !

✎

What sort of jumpers do cows wear ?

Jerseys !

What do you get if you cross a skunk with a balloon?

Something that stinks to high heaven!

What do cats read in the morning?

The Mewspaper!

What did King Kong say when he was told that his sister had had a baby?

I'll be a monkey's uncle!

What did the skunk say when the wind changed direction ?

It's all coming back to me know !

✎

What game do cows play at birthday parties ?

Mooo - sical chairs !

✎

What game do cats play at parties ?

Puss - the - parcel !

What game do fish play at parties ?

Sardines, what else !

What do you get if you cross a hippo with a house sparrow ?

Massive holes in your roof !

Where would you find the skeleton of the very first, prehistoric cow ?

In the Moooo-seum !

What did the sheep say to his girlfriend ?

I Love Ewe !

✎

What did the short sighted hedgehog say to the cactus ?

Oh ! There you are mum !

✎

What do you call a woman with a frog on her head ?

Lily !

✎

What do you get if you cross a cow and a kangaroo ?

Something you need a trampoline to milk !

✎

What is grey, has 4 legs and a trunk ?

A mouse going on holiday !

✎

Did you hear about the stupid farmer who took his cows to the North Pole, thinking he would get ice cream !

What do you get if you cross a chicken with a dog ?

Pooched eggs !

✎

What is the closest thing to silver ?

The Lone Ranger's saddle !

✎

Look at those 50 cows over there !

I said, look at those 50 cows over there !!

Yes, I herd !

What sort of dog is good at looking after children ?

A Baby Setter !

What do the underwater police travel in ?

Squid cars !

Where do birds hold their coffee mornings ?

In a nest-cafe !

What sort of bird has fangs ?

Duckula !

What is hairy and writes ?

A ballpoint ferret !

✎

What do you say to a hitch - hiking frog ?

Hop In !

✎

I think your dog wants my dinner - he keeps jumping up at the table !

Well he didn't eat it this morning when I put it out for him so he'll have to do without now !

What do toads drink?

Croaka Cola!

When do kangaroos propose?

In Leap Years!

Why did the gorilla only eat one computer?

Because he couldn't eat another byte!

What do you call someone who steals sheep?

A Ram Raider!

Why is a real dog better than a cyberpet?

Because your teacher will never believe you if you tell him that your cyberpet buried your homework in the garden!

How does the idiot call his dog ?

He puts both his forefingers in his mouth, takes a deep breath, and shouts 'Here Boy.'

WHAT DO YOU CALL...

What do you call a person made of rubber who stands by the door of a nightclub ?

A Bouncer !

✎

What do you call a vampire singer ?

Fang Sinatra !

✎

What two fish swim across the bed of a lake at 90 miles an hour ?

A Motor Pike and Side Carp !

✎

What do you call a man with a motorcycle hat on in Germany ?

Helmut !

✎

What do you call the river that starred in a cowboy film ?

The Magnificent Severn !

What do you call a woman who juggles pints of beer in a pub ?

Beertrix !

What do you call a bird that goes to college ?

Polly technic !

What do you call a rodent's favourite meal ?

Ratatouille !

What do you call a singing fish?

A sole singer!

✎

What do you call a woman with a parrot on her head?

Polly!

✎

What do you call a woman who works as a bodyguard?

Sal a minder!

What do you call a man who lives just around the corner ?

That's Andy !

✎

What do you call a duck that lives in a teapot ?

A Quackpot !

✎

What do you call a pony with a sore throat ?

A Little Hoarse !

✎

What do you call a rodent with a sword ?

A Mouseketeer !

✎

What do you call a woman with a white face ?

Blanche !

What do you call a sloth's favourite drink ?

Ice cream slowda !

✎

What do you call a woman with two horses ?

Gi - Gi !

✎

What do you call a smelly giant gorilla ?

King Pong !

✎

What do you call a posh car for butchers ?

A Sausage Rolls !

✎

What do you call a dog that likes doing puzzles ?

A lab-rynth !

(An amazing breed !)

What do you call a man who never pays for his food?

Bill!

✎

What do you call a Roman leader with a cold?

Julius Sneezer!

✎

What do you call a dog that wears shorts?

A Boxer!

✎

What do you call a machine that works out how many pockets you have?

A Pocket Calculator!

✎

What do you call a snake with a pocket calculator?

An Adder!

What do you call a pig with fangs?

A hampire!

What do you call a pig that acts in Shakespeare plays?

Hamlet!

What do you call the jewels that ghosts wear?

Tomb stones!

What do you call a woman who has lots of men at her feet ?

A chiropodist !

✎

What do you call the eating implements used by karate club members ?

Chop sticks !

✎

What do you call a mushroom who has lots of fun at parties ?

A Fungi !

✎

What do you call a vicar on a motorbike ?

Rev !

✎

What do you call the instruments made from people's insides that monsters play ?

Organs !

What do you call a man with a clock in the shape of the moon ?

A Lunartick !

✎

What do you get if you cross a chicken with a dog ?

Pooched eggs !

✎

What do you call an elephant crossed with an insect ?

Forget - me - gnat !

✎

What do you call keep fit for ghosts ?

Exorcise !

✎

What do you call an ancient Egyptian who's crumbling ?

A Crummy Mummy !

What do you call a dog that can operate a farmer's 4 wheel drive?

A Land Rover!

What do you call a ghostly teddy bear?

Haunted!

What do you call a pale teddy bear?

Wanted!

What do you call a sun tanned teddy bear ?

Unwanted !

✎

What do you call a rock climbing teddy bear ?

Mounted !

✎

What do you call a teddy bear that's been knocked down by a car ?

Dented !

✎

What do you call a sweet smelling teddy bear ?

Scented !

What do you call a happy teddy bear ?

Contented !

✎

What do you call a teddy bear left at the altar ?

Jilted !

✎

What do you call a teddy bear that serves in Parliament ?

Elected !

✎

What do you call Long John Silver's younger brother ?

Short John Silver !

✎

What does a whale call the youngest member of the family ?

Her baby blubber !

What do you call two rows of cabbages ?

A dual cabbageway !

✎

What do you call a worm rich enough to buy a fur jacket ?

A Caterpillar !

✎

What do you call a wig for a rabbit ?

A Harepiece !

✎

What do you call a popular woman who stays out in the sun for far too long ?

The Toast Of The Town !

✎

What do you call someone whose dad is a cannon ?

A son of a gun !

What do you call the person who delivers mail to a football club ?

The goal-post-man !

What do you call a telephone call from one vicar to another ?

A Parson to Parson call !

What do you call an Owl that robs the rich and gives to the poor ?

Robin Hoot !

What do you call a Scotsman who knows everything?

Ken!

What do you call a hippo at the South Pole?

Lost!

What do you call the stuff that space aliens put on their cakes?

Star - zipan!

What do you call a homeless snail?

A slug!

✎

What do you call a Welsh comedian?

Dai Laughing!

✎

What do you call the very earliest spaceship?

A Dinosaucer!

✎

What do you call the woman who fell off the cliff?

Eileen Dover!

✎

What do you call the man walking on dried leaves?

Russell!

What do you call a man who can't swim ?

Bob !

✎

What do you call a woman who walks around lost ?

Wanda !

✎

What do you call a vegetable that goes camping ?

A boy sprout !

✎

What do you call a film about wildfowl ?

A Duckumentary !

✎

What do you call the job of making nun's clothes ?

Habit forming !

What do you call a a lorry full of feet ?

A toe truck !

✎

What do you call a snake that crushes wild pigs ?

A boar constrictor !

✎

What do you call an older member of your family who thinks he's a pen ?

Your Bic brother !

✎

What do you call an embarrassed potato ?

A beetroot !

What do you call a vampire's favourite pudding ?

Leeches and Scream !

✎

What do you call a goat's favourite food ?

Alphabutt soup !

✎

What do you call a cross between a dog and a phone ?

A Golden Receiver !

✎

What do you call the place where baby monkeys sleep ?

An Apricot !

✎

What do you call a buffalo that you can wash your hands in ?

A Bison !

What do you call a failed magician's relative ?

His Half-brother !

✎

What do you call a deer that goes out in bad weather ?

A rain-deer !

✎

What do you call a place where cats and dogs go to get new tails ?

A Retailer !

✎

What do you call a bird that loves to play cowboys ?

Wyatt Chirp !

✎

What do you call a horse that a monster eats at 3 a.m. ?

A Nightmare !

What do you call a common alien dog ?

A Moon-grel !

✎

What do you call the leader of a convent who conquers the World ?

Attila the Nun !

✎

What do you call a Russian gardener ?

Ivanhoe !

What do you call the flying machines invented by mummies?

Pharoahplanes!

✎

What do you call the event that undertakers and their ponies go to each year?

The Hearse of the Year Show!

✎

What do you call the method of transport used on the sea bed?

Taxi-crab!

✎

What do you call it when cannibals eat a comedian?

A feast of fun!

✎

What do you call a dog that keeps making a bolt for the door?

Blacksmith!

What do you call a place where you can rent out Dracula ?

Vamp-Hire !

✎

What do you call a noisy alien party ?

A Space Racket !

✎

What do you call the first part of a robot teacher's schoolday ?

Assembly !

What do you call it when a Chinese man visits his dentist ?

Tooth Hurty !

✎

What do you call a man who steals things ?

Rob !

✎

What do you call a burglar who fell in a cement mixer ?

A Hardened Criminal !

✎

What do you call the bird that brings monster babies ?

Frankenstork !

✎

What do you call a frog that allows you to park your car ?

A Parking Kermit !

What do you call a short legged tramp ?

A Low Down Bum !

✎

What do you call it when you flush a lot ?

A Chain Reaction !

✎

What do you call a pig driving a car ?

Road hog !

✎

What do you call a TV programme set round a breakfast table ?

A Cereal !

✎

What do you call something with 8 legs and a terrible voice ?

The School Choir !

What do you call an intelligent insect ?

A Spelling Bee !

✎

What do you call a water otter ?

A Kettle !

✎

What do you call a computer operated sheep ?

A Ram !

✎

What do you call a Norwegian car ?

A Fjord Escort !

✎

What do you call a yellow fruit that sings ?

Banana Mouskouri !

What do you call the barrell of beer that fell on a man without hurting him ?

Light Ale !

✎

What do you call a cat that chases outlaws ?

Posse !

✎

What do you call the place where cats get on the coach ?

The Puss Stop !

✎

What do you call a lazy man in a bakery ?

A Loafer !

What do you call a man who sits in the freezer ?

An Ice Cold Pop !

✎

What do you call a woman who spends all her time in the bookmakers ?

Bette !

✎

What do you call it when you shoot at the alarm clock ?

Killing Time !

✎

What do you call a car that acts in adventure films ?

Harrison Ford !

✎

What do you call the worst player in the school football team ?

The Drawback !

What do you call the nuts that fly around in space ?

Astronuts !

✎

What do you call the place where ghosts go for their holidays ?

The Isle of Fright !

✎

What do you call a crocodile's favourite card game ?

Snap !

✎

What do you call a baby crab ?

A Nipper !

✎

What do you call the ghost that is a member of the Royal family ?

The Prince of Wails !

What do you call a liquid that can never freeze ?

Hot Water !

What do you call an adventurous skeleton ?

Indiana Bones !

What do you call the teacher with no legs, arms or body ?

The Head !

What do you call a man with a seagull on his head and sand at his feet ?

Cliff !

What do you call a man whose father was a Canon?

A Son of a Gun!

What do you call a man with two left feet?

Whatever you like – if he tries to catch you he'll just run round in circles!

What do you call a weekly television programme about people getting washed?

A Soap Opera!

What do you call a flock of birds who fly in formation?

The Red Sparrows!

What do you call a bee who is always complaining?

A Grumble Bee!

What would you call a friend who had an elephant on his head?

A Flatmate!

What do you call a posh pig delivering newspapers ?

Bacon Rind !

What do you call a teacher who makes fireworks ?

A Head Banger !

What do you call a man who drills holes in teapots ?

A Potholer !

What do you call a song played on car horns?

A Car Tune!

What do you call the man who invented a famous car and toilet paper?

Lou Rolls!

What do you call an elephant that has had too much to drink?

Trunk!

What do you call the owner of a tool factory?

The Vice Chairman!

✎

What do you call King Midas when he stars in a James Bond film?

Goldfinger!

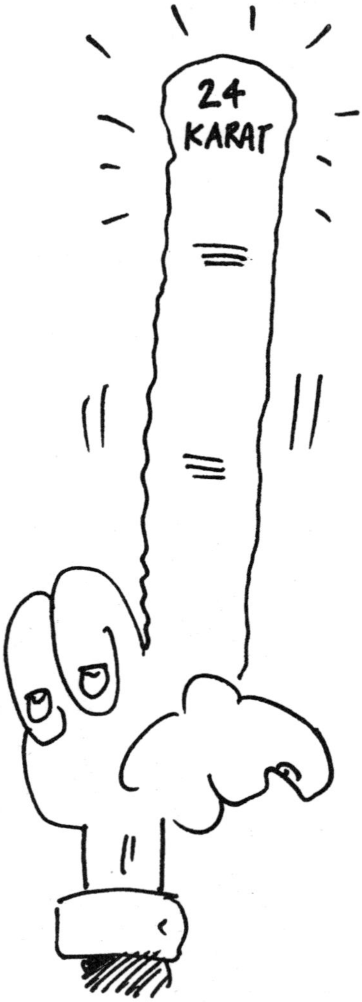

✎

What do you call a parrot when it has dried itself after a bath?

Polly Unsaturated!

✎

What do you call a dentist in the army?

A Drill Sergeant!

What do you call a Kangaroo at the North Pole?

A Lost - Tralien!

What do you call a rabbit dressed up as a cake?

A Cream Bun!

What do you call the man who went to a fancy dress party as a sandwich?

Roland Butter!

What do you call a man who rescues drowning spooks from the sea?

A Ghost Guard!

What do you call someone who makes half size models of fish?

A Scale Modeller!

What do you call someone who draws funny pictures of motor vehicles ?

A Car - Toonist !

✎

What do you call someone who dances on cars ?

A Morris Dancer !

✎

What do you call a fight between film actors ?

Star Wars !

What do you call a group of cars ?

A Clutch !

What do you call a puzzle that is so hard it makes people swear ?

A Crossword !

What do you call a dog that is always getting into fights ?

A Boxer !

What do you call a witch's broomstick when you are very young ?

A Broom Broom !

✎

What do you call a film about Mallards ?

A Duckumentary !

✎

What do you call a musical instrument that is played by two teams of twenty people ?

A Piano Forte !

What do you call a very fast horse ?

Gee Gee Whizz !

✎

What do you call the best dad in the world ?

Top of the Pops !

✎

What do you call a chocolate that teases small animals ?

A Mole - teaser !

✎

What do you call a fish on a motorcycle ?

A Motor Pike !

✎

What do you call a pen with no hair ?

A Bald Point !

What do you call a thing with 22 legs,
11 heads and 2 wings ?

A Football Team !

What do you call a cow that cuts grass ?

A Lawn Moooooer !

What do you call a magical secret agent?

James Wand!

✎

What do you call it when an aeroplane disappears over the horizon?

Boeing, Going, Gone!

✎

What do you call a hearing aid made from fruit?

A Lemonade!

What do you call a policeman with blonde hair ?

A Fair Cop !

✎

What do you call a 5-a-side match played by chimney sweeps ?

Soot Ball !

✎

What do you call a small parent ?

A Minimum !

What do you call a traffic warden who never fines anyone?

A Triffic Warden!

✎

What do you call a telephone call from one vicar to another?

A Parson to Parson call!

✎

What do you call the place where parrots make films?

PollyWood!

What do you call a scared biscuit ?

A Cowardy Custard Cream !

What do you call an Igloo without a toilet ?

An Ig !

What do you call a superb painting done by a rat ?

A Mouseterpiece !

What do you call a box of parrot food ?

Polly Filla !

✎

What do you call it when you pass out after eating too much curry ?

A Korma !

✎

What do you call a chicken that eats cement ?

A Bricklayer !

CRAZY CROSSES

What do you get if you cross a sheep and a space ship?

Apollo Neck Woolly Jumpers!

What do you get if you cross a pig
with a naked person?

Streaky Bacon!

What do you get if you cross a box of
matches and a giant?

The Big Match!

What do you get if you cross a kangaroo with a skyscraper ?

A High Jumper !

What do you get if you cross a road with a safari park ?

Double Yellow Lions !

What do you get if you cross an artist with a policeman ?

A Brush with the Law !

What do you get if you cross an overweight golfer and a pair of very tight trousers ?

A Hole in One !

What do you get if you cross a plumber with a field of cow pats?

The Poohed Piper!

✎

What do you get if you cross an elephant and a bottle of whisky?

Trunk and Disorderly!

✎

What do you get if you cross a flock of sheep and a radiator?

Central Bleating!

What do you get if you cross a skunk and a pair of tennis rackets?

Ping Pong!

What do you get if you cross a pudding and a cow pat?

A Smelly Jelly!

What do you get if you cross a pig and a box of itching powder?

Pork Scratching!

What do you get if you cross a bear with a freezer?

A teddy brrrrrr!

What do you get if you cross a computer with a vampire?

Something new fangled!

What do you get if you cross a tin opener, a vampire and a cricket team?

An opening bat!

What do you get if you cross a cow with a grass cutter?

A lawn mooer!

What do you get if you cross an
ice cream with a dog ?

Frost-bite !

What do you get if you cross a helicopter
with a cornish pasty ?

Something pie in the sky !

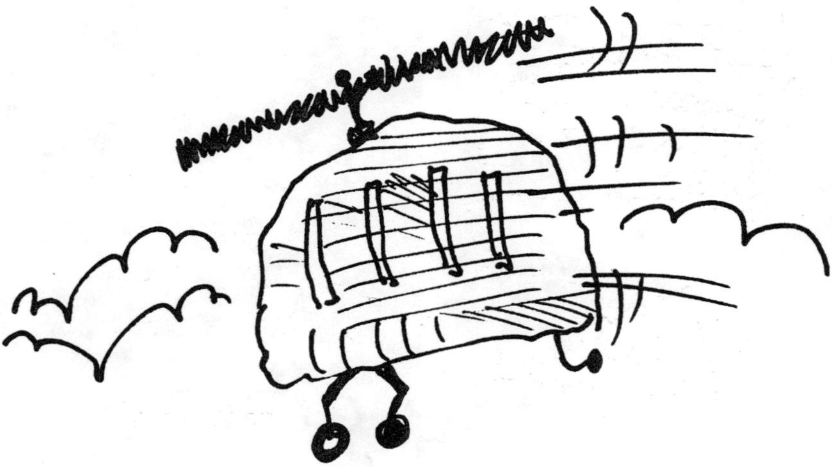

What do you get if you cross a pair of dogs with a
hairdresser ?

A shampoodle and setter !

What do you get if you cross a shoulder bag with a Mallard ?

A Ducksack !

✎

What do you get if you cross a dinosaur with a dog ?

Tyrannosaurus Rex !

✎

What do you get if you cross a football team with a bunch of crazy jokers ?

Mad Jester United !

What do you get if you cross a Viking and a detective ?

Inspector Norse!

What do you get if you cross a large computer and a beefburger ?

A Big Mac !

What do you get if you cross an overheating large computer with a beefburger ?

A Big Mac and Fries !

What do you get if you cross a hat factory and a field of cows ?

A pat on the head !

What do you get if you cross a mouse
and a bottle of olive oil?

A squeak that oils itself!

✎

What do you get if you cross a jogger
with an apple pie?

Puff pastry!

✎

What do you get if you cross a detective with a cat?

A Peeping Tom!

What do you get if you cross a TV programme and a load of sheep ?

A flock-U-mentary !

✎

What do you get if you cross a footballer and a mythical creature ?

A centaur forward !

✎

What do you get if you cross an actress and a glove puppet ?

Sooty and Streep !

What do you get if you cross a pasty and a scary film?

A Cornish Nasty!

✎

What do you get if you cross a pig and a part in a film?

A Ham Roll!

✎

What do you get if you cross a sports reporter with a vegetable?

A Common Tater!

What do you get if you cross a wireless with a hairdresser ?

Radio waves !

What do you get if you cross a hairdresser and a bucket of cement ?

Permanent waves !

What do you get if you cross a toadstool and a full suitcase ?

Not mushroom for your holiday clothes !

What do you get if you cross a dog with a vampire?

A were - woof!

What do you get if you cross a bike and a rose?

Bicycle petals!

What do you get if you cross an alligator and King Midas?

A croc of gold!

What do you get if you cross a tortoise and a storm?

An 'I'm not in a hurry cane!'

What do you get if you cross a chicken with a pod?

Chick peas!

What do you get if you cross a computer with a potato?

Micro chips!

What do you get if you cross a dog with a maze?

A labyrinth!

What do you get if you cross a cow with a crystal ball?

A message from the udder side!

What do you get if you cross a crocodile with a camera?

A snapshot!

What do you get if you cross a chicken and an electricity socket?

A battery hen!

What do you get if you cross a plank of wood and a pencil?

A drawing board!

What do you get if you cross a dog with a football game?

Spot-The-Ball!

What do you get if you cross a spider with a computer?

A web page!

What do you get if you cross a toilet with a pop singer?

Loo - Loo!

✎

What do you get if you cross a frog with a traffic warden?

Toad away!

✎

What do you get if you cross a flea with some moon rock?

A lunar - tick!

What do you get if you cross a vampire and a circus entertainer?

Something that goes straight for the juggler!

What do you get if you cross a snake with a building site?

A boa-constructor!

What do you get if you cross a parrot with an alarm clock?

Politics!

What do you get if you cross a bottle of washing-up liquid and a mouse?

Bubble and squeak!

✎

What do you get if you cross a mountain and a baby?

A cry for Alp!

✎

What do you get if you cross a bunch of flowers with some insects?

Ants in your plants!

What do you get if you cross a bunch of flowers with a burgler ?

Robbery with violets !

✎

What do you get if you cross a cow and a goat ?

Butter from a butter !

✎

What do you get if you cross a pair of hiking boots and a parrot ?

A walkie-talkie !

What do you get if you cross a pen with Napoleon's feet?

A footnote in history!

What do you get if you cross a skunk and a pair of rubber boots?

Smelly wellies!

What do you get if you cross a ghost and an Italian restaurant?

Spookhetti!

What do you get if you cross a cow with an out of date map?

Udderly lost!

What do you get if you cross a TV soap and a rabbit colony ?

Burrow Nation Street !

What do you get if you cross a pelican and a zebra ?

Across the road safely !

What do you get if you cross a bee and a coach ?

A Buzzzz !

What do you get if you cross a monster and a chicken ?

Free strange eggs !

What do you get if you cross a fish and bad breath?

Halibut - osis!

What do you get if you cross a compass and a shellfish?

A guided mussel!

What do you get if you cross a school with a computer supplier?

Floppy desks!

What do you get if you cross a baby with soldiers ?

Infantry !

What do you get if you cross a very bent piece of wood with a spaceship ?

Warp factor 7 !

What do you get if you cross a hairdresser, a storyteller and a young horse ?

A pony tail !

What do you get if you cross a motorcycle and a funny story ?

A Yamaha ha ha ha !

What do you get if you cross a leopard and a bunch of flowers?

A beauty spot!

What do you get if you cross a biscuit with a car tyre?

Crumbs!

What do you get if you cross a rabbit and an aeroplane?

The hare force!

What do you get if you cross a Welshman with a problem?

A Dai - lemma!

What do you get if you cross a pub and a steelworks?

An iron bar!

What do you get if you cross a cow and a jogging machine?

A milk shake!

What do you get if you cross a book and a pound of fat?

Lard of the Rings!

What do you get if you cross a
newsreader and a toad?

A Croaksman!

What do you get if you cross a
ghost and a newsreader?

A Spooksman!

What do you get if you cross a
suitcase with a filbert?

A nut case!

What do you get if you cross a donkey and Christmas ?

Muletide greetings !

✎

What do you get if you cross the devil and an anagram ?

Santa !

✎

What do you get if you cross a Shakespeare play and 3 eggs ?

Omelette !

✎

What do you get if you cross a Shakespeare play and a pig ?

A Ham omelette !

What do you get if you cross a Shakespeare play and a vampire ?

Bat breath !

✎

What do you get if you cross an Eskimo and an ex-boyfriend ?

The cold shoulder !

✎

What do you get if you cross a penguin and an elk ?

Chocolate moose !

What do you get if you cross a chemical and a bicycle ?

Bike carbonate of soda !

✎

What do you get if you cross a skeleton,
a feather and a joke book ?

Rib ticklers !

✎

What do you get if you cross a
skeleton and a garden spade ?

Skullduggery !

What do you get if you cross a skeleton and a dog ?

An animal that buries itself !

What do you get if you cross a skeleton and a tumble drier ?

Bone dry clothes !

What do you get if you cross a fish and a Yamaha ?

A motor pike !

What do you get if you cross a radio music presenter with Match of the Day ?

DDDDDDDDDDDDDDJ!

What do you get if you cross teeth with candy ?

Dental floss !

What do you get if you cross a Spice Girl with a pudding ?

A Jelly Baby !

What do you get if you go on a blind date wearing football boots ?

Stud up !

✎

What do you get if you cross a mad man and a bakery ?

Doughnuts !

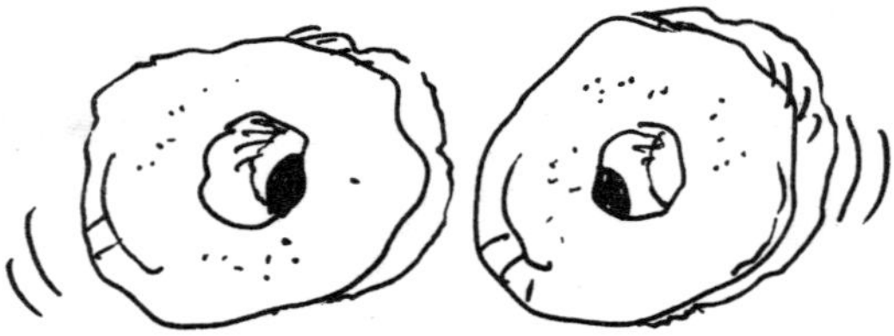

✎

What do you get if you cross a vampire and a bowl of soup ?

Scream of Tomato !

✎

What do you get if you cross a pig and a laundry ?

Hogwash !

What do you get if you cross a cake and a disco ?

Abundance !

What do you get if you cross a bad tempered witch doctor, a fizzy drink and your dad ?

A bottle of pop !

What do you get if you cross a dog and a film studio ?

Collie - wood !

What do you get if you cross an insect and a dance ?

A cricket ball !

What do you get if you cross a giant ape and a self defence class ?

Kong - Fu !

What do you get if you cross a jet engine and a tennis racket ?

A Tennis Rocket !

What do you get if you cross a sheep with a holiday resort ?

The Baaahaaamaaas !

What do you get if you cross a sheep and a vampire ?

A Were - wool !

What do you get if you cross a king and a boat ?

King Canoe !

✎

What do you get if you cross a herb and Doctor Who ?

A Thyme Machine !

✎

What do you get if you cross two sailors and a bottle of HP ?

Tartare Sauce !

What do you get if you cross a telephone and a marriage bureau?

A Wedding Ring!

What do you get if you cross a doctor's surgery and a mountain range?

Peak Practice!

What do you get if you cross a pig and an emergency vehicle?

A Hambulance!

What do you get if you cross a joke book and a snowstorm?

Corn Flakes!

What do you get if you cross a pig and a telephone ?

A lot of crackling on the line !

✎

What do you get if you cross a vampire and a plumber ?

A drain in the neck !

✎

What do you get if you cross an Italian landmark and a ghost ?

The screaming tower of Pisa !

What do you get if you cross a vampire with a mummy?

Something you wouldn't want to unwrap!

✎

What do you get if you cross a carrier pigeon with a woodpecker?

A bird that knocks before delivering a message!

✎

What do you get if you cross a frog and a secret agent?

A croak and dagger story!

What do you get if you cross a jellyfish and an aircraft ?

A jelly copter !

What do you get if you cross a naked woman and the bottom of the ocean ?

A deep sea Lady Godiva !

What do you get if you cross a singer and a tall ladder ?

Someone who can easily get the high notes !

What do you get if you cross a
student and an alien?

Something from another universe - ity!

What do you get if you cross an
alien and a hot drink?

Gravi - tea!

What do you get if you cross a
mummy and a spaceship?

Tutankha - moon!

What do you get if you cross a
gorilla and a prisoner?

A Kong - vict!

ODDS AND EVENS

Knock, knock...
Who's there?
Alison
Alison who?
Alison at your keyhole every day!

✎

Knock, knock...
Who's there?
Jaws
Jaws who?
Jaws truly!

✎

Knock, knock...
Who's there?
Satin
Satin who?
Satin a chair and it collapsed!

✎

Knock, knock...
Who's there?
Midas
Midas who?
Midas well open the door and find out!

Knock, knock...
Who's there?
Renata
Renata who?
Renata sugar - can I borrow a cup?

Knock, knock...
Who's there?
Isadore
Isadore who?
Isadore on the right way round?

Knock, knock...
Who's there?
Don
Don who?
Don be afraid...look into my eyes...you are feeling sleepy!

Knock, knock...
Who's there ?
Bert
Bert who ?
Bert you'll never guess !

✎

Knock, knock...
Who's there ?
Jemima
Jemima who ?
Jemima coming round for a chat ?

✎

Knock, knock...
Who's there ?
Amos
Amos who ?
Amos be going mad – I've come to the wrong house !

✎

Knock, knock...
Who's there ?
Caesar
Caesar who ?
Caesar jolly good fellow....

Knock, knock...
Who's there ?
Arthur
Arthur who ?
Arthur minute and I'll show you my ID card !

Knock, knock...
Who's there ?
Derek
Derek who ?
Derek get richer and the poor get poorer...!

Knock, knock...
Who's there ?
Isaac
Isaac who ?
Isaac you if you don't report into work right now !

Knock, knock...
Who's there ?
Nige
Nige who ?
Nige to see you, to see you Nige !

✎

Knock, knock...
Who's there ?
Alma
Alma who ?
Alma lone out here - open up !

✎

Knock, knock...
Who's there ?
Saul
Saul who ?
Saul the same to me !

Knock, knock...
Who's there ?
Belinda
Belinda who ?
Belinda few ingredients together and make a cake !

✎

Knock, knock...
Who's there ?
Roman
Roman who ?
Roman roads are always straight !

✎

Knock, knock...
Who's there ?
Harpie
Harpie who ?
Harpie holiday !

✎

Knock, knock...
Who's there ?
Seth
Seth who ?
Seth this is how you treat your oldest friend !

Knock, knock...
Who's there ?
Wanda
Wanda who ?
Wanda how long you'll keep me waiting this time !

Knock, knock...
Who's there ?
Eddie
Eddie who ?
Eddie body in dere want by cold ?

Knock, knock...
Who's there ?
Theodore
Theodore who ?
Theodore is locked !

Knock, knock...
Who's there ?
Woof
Woof who ?
Woof, woof, woof, woof, woof....
(Oh, it's the dog !)

✎

Knock, knock...
Who's there ?
Stan
Stan who ?
Stan back, I'm going to break down the door !

✎

Knock, knock...
Who's there ?
Timon
Timon who ?
Timon time again I've told you not to ask that !

✎

Knock, knock...
Who's there ?
Phil
Phil who ?
Phil her up - and check the oil !

Knock, knock...
Who's there?
Barbie
Barbie who?
Barbie couldn't come so he sent me in his place!

✎

Knock, knock...
Who's there?
Dustin
Dustin who?
Dustin time for tea I hope...?

✎

Knock, knock...
Who's there?
Cora
Cora who?
Cora big bird just flew over your house!

✎

Knock, knock...
Who's there?
Scarlet
Scarlet who?
Scarlet a day shall we!

Knock, knock...
Who's there ?
Pierre
Pierre who ?
Pierre through the letterflap !

✎

Did you hear about the monster who went to a holiday camp ?

He won the knobbly knees contest - with his face !

✎

What is dogma ?

A female dog that's had puppies ?

"Are you really going to leave school at the end of this term, Samantha,

or are you just saying it to cheer me up?"

"Now I know there is a link between TV and violence!"

"How did you come to that conclusion?"

"I told my teacher that I watched TV instead of doing my homework last night and she hit me!"

"Harry, why have you got a piano in the bathroom ?"

"Because I'm playing chamber music !"

✎

What kind of jazz do witches like best ?

Hagtime !

✎

The water in our house is musical –

It's always piping hot !

✎

If you forget to do your homework for
our music teacher,

You'll soon find yourself in serious treble !

✎

What is the easiest way to double your money ?

With a pair of scissors !

Why did the man walk around with his umbrella open upside down ?

He heard that there was going to be some change in the weather !

✎

Why did the landlord of the pub have his cash helmet on ?

In case anyone started throwing their money around !

✎

What did the short sighted hedgehog say to the cactus ?

"Ah, there you are dad !"

✎

What do you call an insect at a sale ?

A Jumble Bee !

✎

Why was the chef so relaxed ?

He had plenty of thyme on his hands !

What do you call a happy mushroom ?

Fun Gus !

✎

What happened to the Scottish cat that ran into the road without looking ?

It was kilt !

✎

How long do you want your pyjamas ?

From about October to April !

What can be right but never wrong ?

The angles of a triangle !

✎

What is the noisiest sport ?

Tennis - what a racket !

✎

What is black and white and red in parts ?

A sunburnt penguin !

✎

What animal wears a long coat in the Winter and pants in the Summer ?

A dog !

✎

There's no ham in this ham and mushroom pie !

And there's no cottage in the cottage pie either !

"I think I just swallowed a chicken bone!"

"Are you choking?"

"No, I'm serious!"

Why don't you go outside and play football with your little brother?

I'd rather use a proper football!

What do you get if you jump in the River Nile with bright red swimming trunks on?

Wet!

Roman soldier – "What's the time ?"

Another Roman soldier – "XVII past IX !"

How do ponies send secret messages ?

By horse code !

What sort of dog is used for sniffing out potatoes ?

A spud hound !

Why do you call your dog camera ?

Because it is always snapping at me !

What did the Eskimo girl do to get rid of her boyfriend ?

She gave him the cold shoulder !

What punishment do Eskimo children never have to suffer at school ?

Sitting in the corner !

Who held the baby octopus to ransom ?

Squidnappers !

What do you get if you cross a tin of baked beans with a birthday cake ?

A cake that blows out its own candles !

What is goulash ?

A cremated ghost !

✎

Who won the monster beauty contest ?

Nobody !

✎

My brother has a balanced diet -
he has a can of cola in each hand !

✎

Can you lend me 20p - I want to phone a friend !

Here's 40p - phone them all !

✎

What did the pig say to the farmer ?

You take me for grunted !

Why don't parents like their children to go near chickens?

Because of their fowl language!

✎

Why did the farmer give his chickens a hot water bottle?

He wanted them to lay hard boiled eggs!

✎

Why are you wearing a wet shirt?

Because the label says 'wash and wear'!

Why did the idiot make a hole in his umbrella ?

So that he could tell when it stopped raining !

✎

Why are you home from school so early ?

I was sent home because my best friend was smoking !

But if your best friend was smoking -
why were YOU sent home ?

Because I was the one who set him on fire !

✎

Did you hear about the plastic surgeon who fell asleep in front of the fire - and melted ?

✎

Can Steve come out to play ?

No, he's poorly in bed !

Well, can his cricket bat and ball come out to play ?

What game do monsters play at parties ?

Haunt the thimble !

What did the little monster say after he had been eaten by the big monster ?

It's a little dark, but not as damp as my last flat !

Why did Manchester United want to sign Halley's Comet ?

Because they wanted a shooting star !

What does it mean if a monster's head lights up ?

That he's just had a bright idea !

What kind of coat will keep you warm in Winter ?

A Blazer !

How do you spell mouse trap using only 3 letters ?

C A T !

What did the postage stamp say to the envelope ?

Stick with me and we'll go places !

I'd love to have your photo
And hang it in the shed
To frighten all the rats away
And scare the spiders dead

Little Miss Muffet
Sat on her tuffet
Eating her kippers and spam
Along came a spider
And sat down beside her
So she ate that too, sprinkled with jam

✎

A man was seen putting all the chairs from the park into a lorry.

When someone asked him what he was doing he replied...

"I'm making a band stand!"

✎

FAMOUS LAST WORDS....

What does this button do?

Of course it's not gas, pass me a match and I'll show you!

There hasn't been a train along this line since 1965!

Listen, I know poison when I taste it!

Of course I've taken the fuse out!

What did the monster have after his parents bought him a saw for his birthday ?

Lots of half brothers and sisters !

✎

Why are you hitting your head against the wall ?

My hat is too large, so I'm trying to make my head swell to fit !

✎

Is this the way to the railway station ?

You're certainly on the right track !

✎

How long will the next train be ?

89 metres !

✎

What do monsters do if they have naughty children on their holiday flight ?

Put them outside to play !

What happened to the vampire
with bad breath ?

**His dentist told him to gargoyle
twice a day !**

✎

Why should you not go down to the
woods today ?

Because it's the teddy scares picnic !

✎

Where do aliens leave their spaceships ?

At a parking meteor !

✎

A biology teacher from Leeds

Once swallowed a packet of seeds

A bright orange rose

Grew out of his nose

And his hair was a tangle of weeds !

For your homework I asked you to read Treasure Island, have you done that ?

No, Miss, the video shop was closed !

✎

What was written on the robot's tombstone ?

Rust in pieces !

✎

How does a snowman travel around ?

By icicle !

✎

What is black, crazy and nests in a tree ?

A Raven lunatic !

✎

Why is a bad golfer like an outboard motor ?

Because they both go putt, putt, putt, putt, putt....

What did the gun say to the bullet ?

You're fired, get out of here !

✎

What do reindeer say before they start telling you a joke ?

This one will sleigh you !

✎

How did the snowman feel when he had a bad cold ?

Abominable !

Sardines really are the most stupid fish of all !

Why do you say that ?

They lock themselves into little cans, and then leave the key outside !

✎

A man was shovelling snow from his front pathway when a neighbour walked past.

"You're doing it the hard way, why not just burn it away ?"

The man thought long and hard about this then replied,

"but then I'd have to shovel all the ashes away !"

✎

What is black and white and can't turn round in a narrow space ?

A nun carrying a snooker cue !

I think I've got chicken pox!

What makes you think it's chicken pox?

Because I feel peckish!

What do you get if you cross a vampire and a jar of peanut butter?

A vampire that sticks to the roof of your mouth!

"I'm sorry, Mr Smith, but I think you have rabies!"

"In that case give me a piece of paper and a pen!"

"Are you going to write your will?"

"No, a list of all the people I want to bite!"

"Mummy, mummy, Charles has broken my favourite Doll!"

"How did he do that?"

"When I hit him over the head with it!"

✎

"When I grow up I want to be a ballet dancer!"

"That's a job that will keep you on your toes!"

"Dad, do you have a good memory for faces ?"

"I think so, son, why do you ask ?"

"Because I've just broken your shaving mirror !"

✎

My dog loves to fly !

He's a jet setter !

✎

What did the old man do when he thought he was dying ?

He moved his bed into the living room !

✎

"Please use the word 'information' in a sentence."

"Sometimes birds fly information !"

✎

"What makes you think I'm stupid ?"

"Well, when you went to that mind reader she only charged you half price !"

Which pets are the noisiest ?

Trumpets !

✎

"I'd like two slices of steak, and make them lean !"

"Certainly, sir, which way ?"

✎

Did you hear about the man who thought the Rover 3.5 was a robotic dog ?

✎

What happened to the robot who fell off the fireplace ?

He was dismantled !

✎

"Doctor, I've got double vision !"

"Well close one eye !"

What do you get if you cross a monster with a cat ?

No more stray dogs for at least a 2 mile radius !

✎

What is the difference between a burglar and a man in a wig ?

One has false keys, the other has false locks !

✎

Where are famous monsters buried ?

In Westmonster Cathedral !

✎

Your daughter has the ability to really go places and, as her teacher, I can't wait !

✎

Our Art teacher draws her own conclusions !

✎

What trees are deck chairs made from ?

Beach trees !

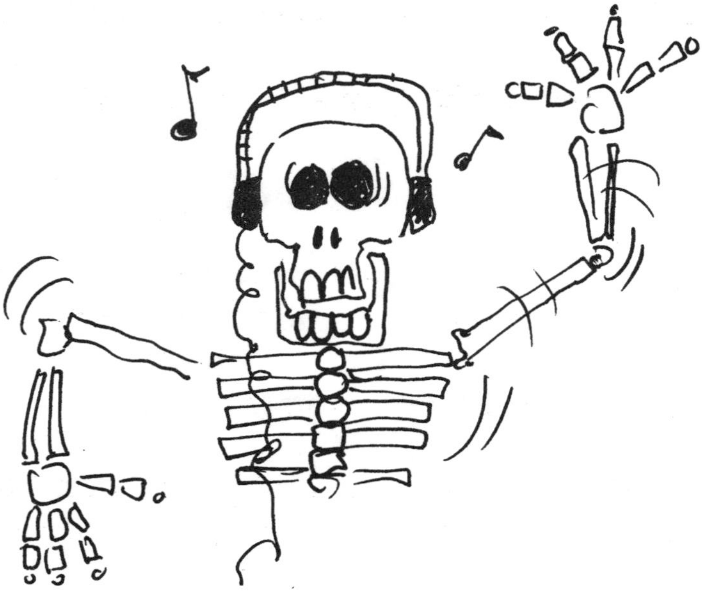

How do skeletons listen to tapes ?

On their bony walkmans !

✎

How can you tell that owls are wiser than chickens ?

Have you ever seen a Kentucky Fried Owl ?

✎

What do you get if you travel in a space ship with a toad ?

Star Warts !

Why did the man have a sausage stuck behind his ear ?

Because he'd just eaten his pencil !

✎

When German cars retire
- do they go to the old Volks home ?

✎

If Superman is so clever, why does he wear his underpants on the outside of his trousers !

✎

How can you tell when a train has just been past ?

They always leave tracks !

✎

How can you tell if there's an elephant in the fridge ?

You can't shut the door !

✎

How do you communicate with a fish ?

Drop it a line !

I used to be big headed - but now I'm perfect !

✎

I never read books by Tolkien -

They are much too Hobbit forming !

✎

You should never hit a man while he's down...

...he just might get up again and hit you back !

✎

"Blenkinsop, why have you come to school wearing only one glove ?"

"Because the weather forecast said that on the one hand it might be warm, but on the other hand it might be cool !"

✎

Where do frogs and toads hang their coats ?

In the croak room !

Why are brides so unlucky ?

They never marry the best man !

✎

Why should you never climb aboard an alien space craft ?

Because you might just get carried away !

✎

What is white on the outside, black and green on the inside and slippery when you eat it ?

A slug and lettuce sandwich !

✎

How do monsters get across the sea ?

On a cross channel furry !

✎

Why did the burglar saw the legs off his bed ?

Because he wanted to lie low for a while !

"Waiter this omelette tastes awful!"

"Sir, I can assure you that our chef has been making omelettes since he was a child!"

"That may be true - but can I have one of his fresher ones please?"

✎

What do you call a fat space alien?

An Extra - cholesterol!

✎

What has four legs and flies?

Two pairs of trousers!

Or

Two witches on a broomstick!

✎

I'm terribly homesick!

But this is your home!

I know, and I'm sick of it!

I hear the monster executioner got a job in a department store?

Yes, he's now the Head Buyer!

How can you tell when a mummy is angry?

It flips its lid!

Our needlecraft teacher is a real sew and sew !

What did the mummy burglar say when he was found not guilty ?

"I beat the wrap !"

What do you call a hippo that wears flowers in its hair and a string of beads around its neck ?

A Hippie - potamous !

Why did the stupid thief fly through the jewellers shop window ?

He forgot to let go of the brick !

Why did the driver reverse up the motorway in the wrong direction ?

Because he knew the rules of the road backwards !

A burglar tried to hold up a bank but found that he had brought his teddy bear instead of a gun.

What was he charged with ?

Assault with a teddly weapon !

✎

What do you get if a cat sits on a beach at Christmas ?

Sandy claws !

✎

What sort of glasses do ghosts wear ?

Spooktacles !

BATTY BOOKS – READ THEM NOW...

How to be a Great Gardener

By
Teresa Green

The Parachute Tester

By
Hugo Furst

Fishing From The Beach

By
C. Shaw

The Ghost Hunters

By
Terry Fied

Running A Guest House

By
Chris P Bacon

The Fall From The Cliff Top

By
Eileen Dover

How To Make Your Own Desserts

By
I. Scream

A Holiday Abroad

By
Frances Close

My Criminal Life

By
Robin Banks

Living Life In The Nude

By
Major Stare

What do you know about the Dead Sea?

I didn't even know it had been ill!

Water - a colourless and odourless liquid,

that turns brown and smelly when I put my feet in it!

Two boys were fighting in the street. An old lady separated them and gave them a telling off.

"You should learn a bit of give and take," she said.

"I have," replied one boy, "I gave him a thump because he took my walkman!"

✎

A bowl of lasagne walked into a pub and ordered a drink.

"Sorry," said the barmaid, "we don't serve food after 2 o'clock!"

✎

What shall I do with all this soil I've got after digging this hole?

Just dig another hole and bury it!

✎

Do you always take a bath in such filthy water?

It wasn't filthy when I got in!

What is black and white and black and white....

A nun rolling down a hill !

✎

Did you hear about the boy who thought he was Dracula ?

He was a real pain in the neck !

✎

Dad - there's a man here collecting for the old folks home ?

Give him your Gran !

✎

Which rich Arab invented crisps ?

Sultan Vinegar !

Who are the rudest creatures in the farmyard ?

Chickens - they are always using fowl language !

What do you call two spiders who have just got married ?

Newly Webs !

Knock, Knock...
Whos's there ?
Arthur !
Arthur Who ?
Arthur any more biscuits left - I'm still hungry !

What do astronauts cook their eggs and bacon in ?

An Unidentified Frying Object !

What are moonbeams ?

Things that hold the moon up ?

Why did the monster stick a cartoonist up his nose when he had a cold?

Because toons help you breathe more easily!

✎

Blenkinsop - I've told you before - stop acting like an idiot!

But, sir, I'm not acting!

✎

An astronaut and a chimp were fired off into space. The chimp opened its sealed orders and, as it read them it started pushing buttons and programming the flight computer.
When the astronaut opened his sealed orders he found only one sentence...

"Feed the chimp!"

✎

What do you get if a post office burns down?

Black mail!

Why do we have lips ?

To stop our mouths fraying at the edges !

This coffee is disgusting – it tastes like mud !

I'm not surprised – it was ground a few minutes ago !

My music teacher said I have a heavenly voice !

That's not strictly true – she said your voice was like nothing on Earth !

Last night someone made a hole in the fence around the local nudist camp!

The local police are looking into it round the clock!

✎

Did you hear about the idiot who invented a new spray to kill garden insects?

You spray it on all your plants - it kills them all stone dead - so the insects starve!

✎

Where do nudist comedians get all their jokes?

They employ stripped writers!

✎

Blenkinsop - you weren't in school last Friday, and I understand from some of your classmates that you were, in fact, at a disco!

That's not true, Miss, and I still have the cinema tickets to prove it!

Did you hear about the man who decided to complain about the food in a Chinese restaurant. He called over the waiter...

"That steak was rubbery!"

"Thank you for the compliment, sir, and have a rubbery evening!"

✎

Did you hear about the idiot who wrote himself a letter, forgot to sign it and then, when it arrived, couldn't work out who it was from!

✎

Darling – your cheeks are like petals – bicycle petals...

Your teeth are like stars – they come out at night...

Your skin is like a million dollars – all green and crinkly!

✎

Which ghost haunts the 3 bears?

Ghouldilocks!

How do aliens go fishing ?

With earthworms !

✎

What is the capital of Australia ?

A !

✎

Why was the little girl wrapped up in bandages ?

Because she was mummy's little pet !

✎

How do you know when a cannibal fancies eating you ?

He keeps buttering you up !

✎

What sort of wine do cannibals like best ?

One with plenty of body in it !

Can I share your skis ?

Sure - you have them going uphill, and I'll have them going down !

✎

What lives in a forest and tells the dullest stories ever heard ?

A wild boar !

✎

How does Frankenstein's monster sit in a chair ?

Bolt upright !

What did the giant spider from outer space build ?

A World Wide Web !

✎

What do you say when you meet a toad ?

Wart's new with you !?

✎

When is a car like a frog - when it's being toad away !

✎

What sort of bull doesn't have horns ?

A Bullfrog !

✎

Which fish can only be seen at night ?

A Starfish !

✎

Which TV station do werewolves watch ?

Channel Fur !

Where is the only place on Earth where Friday comes before Thursday ?

A Dictionary !

✎

What sort of can can you set light to ?

A candle !

✎

Why did the body builder rub grease onto his muscles at bedtime ?

He needed to be oily the next morning !

✎

That good looking boy over there is getting on my nerves !

But he's not even looking at you ?

That's what is getting on my nerves !

Teacher - I hope I didn't see you cheating then, Blenkinsop !

Blenkinsop - I hope you didn't see me cheating either, Miss !

✎

Hey, look at this great wallet full of cash that I found in the street !

Are you sure it's lost ?

Certainly - I had to wait 20 minutes until the man had finished looking for it before I could pick it up from under my shoe !

✎

What do you call a fox in trouble with the police ?

A brush with the law !

✎

What do you call a new, super cat ?

A Mew Improved Version !

Did you hear about the meanest man in the World?

...He found a pair of crutches on a train, and went home and broke his brothers leg!

...When I saw him stripping the wallpaper in his house I said I didn't know he was redecorating - He said he wasn't redecorating - he was moving house!

...he took up passive smoking to save money!

...he pinched this book from a friend instead of buying his own copy!

What do you call a man with a tree growing out of his head?

Ed - Wood!

✎

What do you call a woman with a sheep on her head?

Baa - Baa - Ra!

✎

What do you call a man who wears tissue paper trousers?

Russell!

What do you call a nun with a washing machine on her head?

Sister Matic!

Why did the man with a pony tail go to see his doctor?

He was a little hoarse!

What do you call a witch flying through the skies?

Broom Hilda!

How did the Prime Minister get to know the secret?

Someone Blairted it out!

What did the idiot call his pet zebra?

Spot!

What do you call a fish on the dining table ?

A Plaice Mat !

✎

What do you call a man made from toilet paper ?

Louie !

✎

What do you call a very tidy woman ?

Anita House !

✎

What do you call a vampire that can lift up cars ?

Jack - u - la !

Who gets the sack as soon as he starts work ?

A postman !

What do you call a vampire Father Christmas ?

Sack - u - la !

What do you call a girl who lives on the same street as a vampire ?

The girl necks door !

What do you call a picture painted by an old master ?

An Old Masterpiece !

✎

What do you call a horse that eats Indian food ?

Onion Bha - gee - gee !

✎

What do you call a vegetable that tells jokes ?

Jasper Carrot !

✎

What do you call the coldest mammal in the World ?

The Blue Whale !

What do you call a dog that makes a bolt for the door ?

Blacksmith !

✎

What do you call a man who steals cows ?

A beef burgler !

✎

What do you call a man with a pile of soil on his head ?

Doug !

✎

What do you call a man after he has
washed the soil off his head ?

Douglas !

What do you call a girl at a railway station?

Victoria!

✎

How does Posh Spice keep her husband under control?

He's at her Beckham call!

✎

What do you call an overweight vicar who plays football?

The roly - poly - holy - goalie!

What do you call a woman with sandpaper on her head?

Sandie!

What do you call her sister who lives at the seaside?

Sandie Shaw!

What do you call the largest computer you can buy?

A Big Mac!

What do you call medicine for horses?

Cough stirrup!

What do you call a pretend railway?

A play station!

What do you call a man with a kilt over his head?

Scott!

✎

What do you call a man with a pig on his head?

Hamlet!

✎

What do you call a man with eggs on his head?

Omelette!

✎

What do you shout to the Frenchman
at the back of the race?

Camembert!

What do you call a poster advertising the last teddy for sale in the shop ?

A one ted poster !

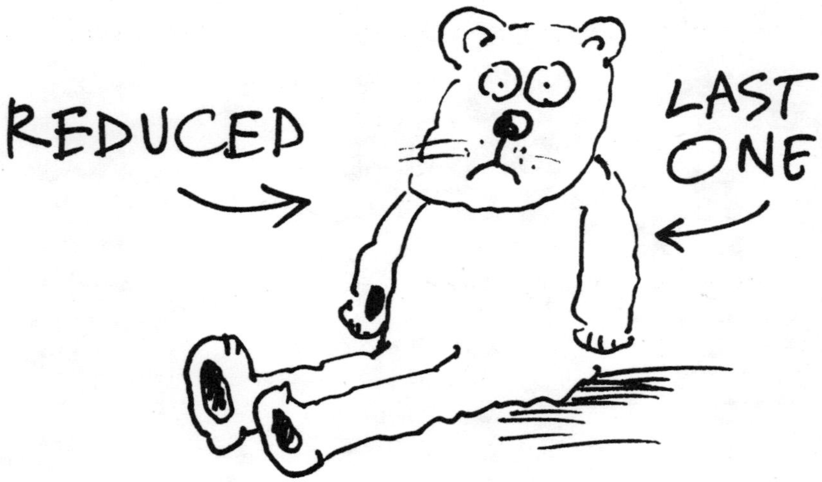

✎

What do you call the dance that grown ups do in the supermarket ?

The can-can !

✎

What do you call a DJ lying across a horse's back ?

Jimmy Saddle !

What do you call a girl with a supermarket checkout on her head?

Tilly!

✎

What do you call a mummy that washes up?

Pharaoh liquid!

✎

What do you call a Scottish racehorse rider?

Jock - ey!

✎

What do you call a pig with an itch?

Pork scratching!

What do you call a rodent's carpet ?

A mouse mat !

✎

What do you call a sweater that bounces ?

A Bungee Jumper !

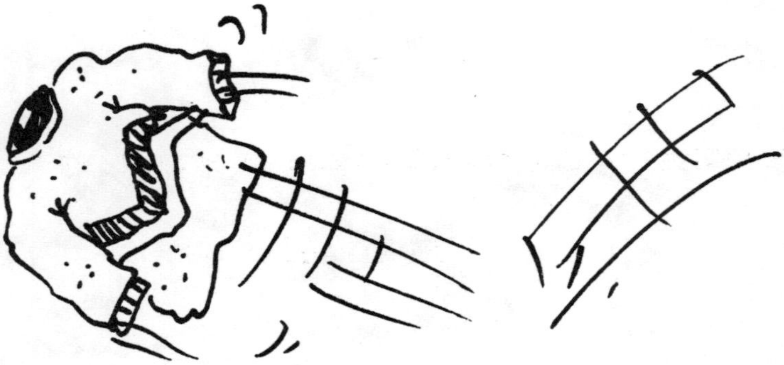

✎

How do you spell hungry horse using just 4 letters ?

M T G G !

✎

What do you call a woman dressed up as a gang of motor repairers ?

Car - men !

What do you call a Welshman who writes lots of letters ?

Pen Gwyn !

What sort of food can you get in a pub run by sheep ?

Baaa meals !

What do you call a female magician ?

Trixie !

What do you call well repaired holes in socks ?

Darned good !

What do you call a group made up of animal doctors ?

Vet, vet, vet !

What do you call a woman with a beach on her head ?

Shelly !

What do you call a postman with a cow on his head ?

Pat !

What do you call a woman who goes horse racing ?

Betty !

What do you call a woman who works in a bakers ?

Bunty !

✎

What do you call a dinosaur that drinks PG Tips ?

A Tea Rex !

✎

What do you call a deaf monster ?

Whatever you like - he can't hear you !

✎

What do you call a vampire pig ?

Pork-U-La !

✎

What do you call a man with a collection of fish photographs ?

The Prints of Whales !

(Yes, I know they're mammals really, but I liked the joke anyway !)

What do you call a man with this book on his head?

Joe King!

✎

What do you call a man with a football pitch on his head?

Alf Time!

✎

What do you call a man who cleans out toilets?

Lou!

✎

What do you call a man with the word LATER painted on his head?

Ron (Later Ron!)

✎

What do you call a woman with a bicycle on her head?

Petal!

What do you call a woman with a computerised piano on the side of her head?

Cynthia!

What do you call a woman with a computerised piano on top of her head?

Hyacinth!

What do you call a man with a load of sports equipment on his head?

Jim!

What do you call a boy who is always making fun of people ?

Mickey !

✎

What do you call a man with a load of flowers and vegetables growing on his head ?

Gordon !

✎

What do you call a woman that people sit on ?

Cher !

✎

What do you call a man with a spade on his head ?

Digby !

What do you call a woman with a boat on her head ?

Maude !

✎

What do you call a Roman emperor with flu ?

Julius Sneezer !

✎

What do you call a man with a sack full of stolen goods over his shoulder ?

Robin !

✎

What do you call a girl with a star on her head ?

Stella !

What do you call a mad man with the moon on his head?

Lunar Dick!

✎

What do you call a man with seagulls on his head?

Cliff!

✎

What do you call a secret store of food in a monastery?

Friar Tuck

What do you call a man with a swarm of bees round his head?

A. B. Hive!

What do you call a woman with a short skirt on?

Denise!

What do you call a man with debts?

Bill!

What do you call a woman who throws her bills on the fire?

Bernadette!

What do you call a man who is part man, part jungle cat?

Richard the Lion Half!

Why did the girl have a horse on her head ?

Because she wanted a pony tail !

✎

What do you call a man
with a karaoke machine ?

Mike !

✎

What do you call a man who checks the size
of rabbit holes ?

A Burrow Surveyor !

✎

What do you call a woman with a nut tree on her head ?

Hazel !

✎

What do you call a failed lion tamer ?

Claude Bottom !

What do you call a woman with a cat on her head?

Kitty!

What do you call a woman with a food mixer on her head?

Belinda!

What do you call a man who does everything in 30 seconds?

Arthur Minute!

What do you call a woman who is crunchy and thin ?

Crisp - tine !

What do you call a man who swings through the jungle backwards ?

Nazrat !

What do you call a man who keeps chickens ?

Gregory Peck !

What do you call a man with a computer on his head ?

CD Ron !

What do you call a woman with a kettle on her head ?

Tina !

✎

What do you call a disguise worn by an Elk ?

A False Moosetache !

✎

What do you call a robbery in China ?

A Chinese Take Away !

✎

What do you call a cat that is always having accidents ?

A Catastrophe !

✎

What do you call two elephants at the swimming pool ?

A Pair Of Swimming Trunks !

What do you call a dog in a breadcake ?

A Hot Dog !

✎

What do you call a teddies favourite drink ?

Ginger Bear !

✎

What do you call a dance that snowmen go to ?

A Snowball !

✎

What do you call the ring that worms leave round the bath ?

The Scum Of The Earth !

✎

What do you call a sheep that says Moo ?

Bilingual !

What do you call the flour that fairies make bread with ?

Elf Raising Flour !

✎

What do you call the highest form of animal life ?

A Giraffe !

✎

Why did the robber take a bath ?

So he could make a clean get-away !

✎

What do you call a secret agent in a shop ?

A Counter Spy !

What do you call a dog that likes doing experiments ?

A Lab-rador !

✎

What do you call a buffalo that you can wash your hands in ?

A Bison !

✎

What do you call a man who jumps off a cliff with a budgie on each arm ?

A Budgie Jumper !

✎

What do you call the glasses a short sighted ghost wears ?

Spooktacles !

What do you call something that runs around your garden all day and never stops ?

The Fence !

What do you call the place where the Police keep rhubarb thieves ?

Custardy !

What do you call a frog's favourite sweet ?

A Lollihop !

What do you call something that is green and white and hops ?

A Frog Sandwich !

UGH ! That is so sick !

Yes, and so was my dad when he opened his packed lunchbox !

What do you call a holiday resort for bees ?

Stingapore !

What do you call the song that monkeys and elephants sing at Christmas ?

Jungle Bells !

What do you call a snail's favourite clothes ?

A Shell Suit !

✎

What do you call a duck that's been to University ?

A Wise Quacker !

✎

What do you call a baby turkey ?

A Goblet !

What do you call a rocking chair fitted with wheels ?

A Rock - And - Roller !

✎

What do you call a pair of shoes made from banana skins ?

Slippers !

✎

What do you call first aid for an injured lemon ?

Lemonade !

What do you call Tarzan when he visits Mars ?

Marzipan !

✎

What do you call a fish that's eaten 24 carrots ?

A Gold Fish !

✎

What do you call a fish that can't swim ?

Dead !

✎

What do you call the King who invented the fireplace ?

Alfred the Grate !

What do you call a cat that's eaten a lemon ?

A Sourpuss !

What do you say to an angry monster ?

No need to bite my head off !

What do you call the longest night of the year ?

A Fortnight !

What do you call a fast food snack served at a church fete ?

A Hymn Burger !

What do you call a mayfly with criminal tendencies?

Baddy long legs!

What do you call a ghost's songbook?

Sheet Music!

What do you call a person who falls onto you on a bus or train?

A Laplander!

What do you call the World's first foot doctor ?

William the Corncurer !

What do you call a holiday that rabbits go on when they first get married ?

Bunnymoon !

What do you call a bull you can put in the washing machine ?

Washable !

What do you call something purple that swings through vineyards?

Tarzan the grape man!

✎

What do you call a person who shouts all the way through a football match?

A Foot bawler!